Contemporary Irish Writers

Contemporary Irish Writers and Filmmakers

General Series Editor:
Eugene O'Brien, Head of English Department, Mary Immaculate College, University of Limerick.

Titles in the series:

Forthcoming:

Contemporary Irish Writers

Brendan Kennelly

A Host of Ghosts

John McDonagh

To Kate,

good health and happiness

always to you,

Brendan Kennelly

8/5/2004

The Liffey Press

Published by The Liffey Press
Ashbrook House, 10 Main Street,
Raheny, Dublin 5, Ireland.
www.theliffeypress.com

A catalogue record of this book is
available from the British Library.

ISBN 1-904148-44-1

*This book has been published with the assistance of grant-aid
from An Chomhairle Ealaíon, The Arts Council of Ireland*

Printed in the Republic of Ireland by ColourBooks Ltd.

Contents

Conclusion

About the Author

Dr John McDonagh is a lecturer in the Department of English at Mary Immaculate College, University of Limerick. He has published numerous articles on Irish writing in journals such as *The Irish University Review, Studies, Scripture Bulletin* and *Working Papers in Irish Studies*.

Series Introduction

Given the amount of study that the topic of Irish writing, and increasingly Irish film, has generated, perhaps the first task of a series entitled *Contemporary Irish Writers and Filmmakers* is to justify its existence in a time of diminishing rainforests. As Declan Kiberd's *Irish Classics* has shown, Ireland has produced a great variety of writers who have influenced indigenous, and indeed, world culture, and there are innumerable books devoted to the study of the works of Yeats, Joyce and Beckett. These writers spoke out of a particular Irish culture, and also transcended that culture to speak to the Anglophone world, and beyond.

However, Ireland is now a very different place from that which figures in the works of Yeats, Joyce and Beckett, and it seems timely that the representations of this more secular, more European, and more cosmopolitan Ireland should be investigated and it is with this in mind that *Contemporary Irish Writers and Filmmakers* has been launched.

This series will examine the work of writers and filmmakers who have engaged with the contemporary cultural issues that are important in Ireland today. Irish literature and film has often been viewed as obsessed with the past, but contemporary writers and filmmakers seem to be involved in a process of negotiation between the Ireland of the past and the Ireland of the coming times. It is on this process of negotiation that much of our current imaginative literature and film is focused, and this series hopes to investigate this process through the chosen *auteurs*.

Indeed, it is a sign of the maturity of these *auteurs* that many of them base their narratives not only in the setting of this "new Ireland", but often beyond these shores. Writers and filmmakers such as Seamus Heaney, John Banville, William Trevor and Neil Jordan have the confidence to write and work as *artists* without the necessary addendum of the qualifying "Irish". Their concerns, themes and settings take them outside Ireland to a global stage. Yet, as this series attests, their "Irishness", however that is defined, remains intact and is often imprinted even in their most "international" works.

Politically and culturally, contemporary Ireland is in something of a values deficit as the previous hegemonic certainties of party political and religious allegiance have been lost in a plethora of scandals involving church and state. The role of art and culture in redefining the value-ethic for our culture has never been more important, and these studies will focus on the notions of Irishness and identity that prevail in the late twentieth and early twenty-first centuries.

The role of the aesthetic in the shaping of attitudes and opinions cannot be understated and these books will attempt to understand the transformative potential of the work of the artist in the context of the ongoing redefinition of society and culture. The current proliferation of writers and filmmakers of the highest quality can be taken as an index of the growing confidence of this society, and of the desire to enunciate that confidence. However, as Luke Gibbons has put it: "a people has not found its voice until it has expressed itself, not only in a body of creative works, but also in a body of critical works", and *Contemporary Irish Writers and Filmmakers* is part of such an attempt to find that voice.

Aimed at the student and general reader alike, it is hoped that the series will play its part in enabling our continuing participation in the great humanistic project of understanding ourselves and others.

Eugene O'Brien
Department of English
Mary Immaculate College
University of Limerick

Acknowledgements

Firstly, to my wife, Trish, without whose constant and un-wavering support, in every way, this book would not have been written. Huge gratitude is also due to my Head of De-partment at Mary Immaculate College, Eugene O'Brien, whose initial support and encouragement and positive editing were central to the production of the book. I would also like to thank Brian Langan of The Liffey Press whose perceptive reading and comments have made this a better book. Kate, as always, was looking out for us all. Finally, to John, Brigid, Pat-rick and Michael for early mornings, constant questions and hope for the future.

Versions of some of the chapters in this book have ap-peared previously in *Studies* and *The Irish University Review*.

For Trish, John, Brigid, Patrick and Michael

Chronology

1936	17 April, Brendan Kennelly born in Ballylongford, County Kerry
1948–53	Attends Jane Agnes McKenna's school in Tarbert, County Kerry
1957–61	Attends Trinity College, Dublin, where he is awarded a Double First in English and French
1959	*Cast A Cold Eye* (with Rudi Holzapfel)
1961	Awarded double first in English and French BA by Trinity College *The Rain, The Moon* (with Rudi Holzapfel)
1962	*The Dark About Our Loves* (with Rudi Holzapfel)
1963	*Green Townlands* (with Rudi Holzapfel) *Let Fall No Burning Leaf* *The Crooked Cross*
1964	*My Dark Fathers*
1965	*Up and At It*
1966	Awarded PhD by Trinity College *Collection One: Getting Up Early*

1967	Good Souls To Survive The Florentines Wins the AE Memorial Prize for Poetry
1968	Dream of a Black Fox
1969	Selected Poems
1970	A Drinking Cup: Poems from the Irish Edits The Penguin Book of Irish Verse
1971	Bread Selected Poems (enlarged edition)
1972	Love Cry Salvation: The Stranger
1973	The Voices: A Sequence of Poems Appointed Professor of Modern Literature at Trinity College, Dublin
1974	Shelley in Dublin
1975	A Kind of Trust
1976	New and Selected Poems
1977	Islandman: A Poem
1978	A Girl: 22 Songs performed on RTE radio (fully published in Breathing Spaces (1992)) The Visitor
1979	A Small Light: Ten Songs of O'Connor of Carrigafoyle In Spite of the Wise (also titled Evasions)
1980	The Boats Are Home
1982	The House That Jack Didn't Build
1983	Cromwell: A Poem
1984	Moloney Up and At It
1985	Selected Poems

1987	*Mary: From the Irish*
1988	Edits *Landmarks of Irish Drama* Wins Critics' Special Harveys Award
1989	*Love of Ireland: Poems from the Irish*
1990	*A Time for Voices: Selected Poems 1960–1990*
1991	*The Book of Judas* *Euripides' Medea: A New Version*
1992	*Breathing Spaces: Early Poems*
1993	*Euripides' The Trojan Women: A New Version* Edits *Between Innocence and Peace: Favourite Poems of Ireland*
1994	*Journey into Joy: Selected Prose* edited by Åke Persson
1995	*Poetry My Arse*
1996	*Sophocles' Antigone: A New Version* *Lorca's Blood Wedding: A New Version* Edits *Dublines* with Katie Donovan *This Fellow With the Fabulous Smile: A Tribute to Brendan Kennelly* edited by Åke Persson
1998	*The Man Made of Rain* *The Singing Tree*
1999	*Begin*
2001	*Glimpses*
2002	*The Little Book of Judas*
2003	*Martial Art*

List of Abbreviations

Introduction

Leading the Blind

Therefore I accept dark privacy;
I move beyond each voice
Which, unaware, asserts I cannot see.
While they acclaim, reproach, ignore, rejoice,
I go among them, prodding the strange air,
Awkwardly involved while still outside,
Conscious of the things I'm fit to share,
Acknowledging the light I've been denied.
        (From "The Blind Man", *CO*, 35)

While contemporaries such as Seamus Heaney, Derek
Mahon, Eavan Boland and Thomas Kinsella have all attracted a
good deal of both critical acclaim and academic attention,
Brendan Kennelly's extraordinary body of work has, with the
notable exception of a few doctoral theses and an edited col-
lection of critical essays,[1] languished somewhat in the critical
wilderness, despite the fact that his collection *Good Souls to
Survive* pipped Seamus Heaney's first collection *Death of a*

---

[1] Åke Persson's *Betraying the Age: Social and Artistic Protest in Brendan Ken-
nelly's Work* was published by Gothenburg University Press in 2000. This
covers Kennelly's work up to 1996. Erwin Otto's thesis, *Das Lyrische Werk
Brendan Kennelly* was published in 1976 by Peter Lang (Frankfurt am Main).
Also, Richard Pine's edited anthology of critical essays on Kennelly, *Dark
Fathers into Light*, was published by Bloodaxe Books in 1994.

Naturalist for the prestigious AE Memorial Prize for Poetry in
1966. This is even more extraordinary when the huge popu-
larity of the work is considered, with collections such as
Cromwell, The Book of Judas and *The Man Made of Rain* regu-
larly featuring in the bestsellers list. Kennelly's contribution to
the development of contemporary Irish poetry has been and
continues to be immense, and his epic collections are increas-
ingly being regarded as seminal texts in the development of
both twentieth- and twenty-first-century Irish poetry. The
purpose of this book will be to provide a critical introduction
to the broad corpus of Kennelly's work by focusing on the
major works and attempting to draw on the dominant
themes and styles that have concerned Kennelly over the
course of a forty-five-year poetic career.

Brendan Kennelly was born in Ballylongford, County Kerry,
on 17 April 1936. Ballylongford is a crossroads village close to
the mouth of the river Shannon to the north, the Atlantic
Ocean to the west and the rich farmland of the Golden Vale to
the south and east. It is a small village composed of a few
shops, a garage, a church and an unfeasibly large number of
pubs, in many ways an archetypal rural Irish village. Kennelly's
father Tim and his mother Bridie Ahern ran one of these pubs
and Kennelly grew up, along with five brothers and two sisters,
with the singing, storytelling and conversation that epitomised
the public house at the centre of the social and cultural life of
the village. Interestingly, John B. Keane refers to Ballylongford
as a town (Persson, 1996: 61), intimating perhaps a more com-
plex socio-cultural environment than the implied simplicity of a
village, and this complexity can be seen in Kennelly's varied and
often contradictory poetic responses to his experience of
growing up in such a close-knit yet introspective community.

There are strong parallels between Kennelly's unromanti-
cised, spare and often harsh portrayal of his community and
the poetry of Patrick Kavanagh in the early 1940s, with both
clearly displaying a natural empathy with, and deep under-

standing of, their respective birthplaces, although the poetic desire to see beneath and beyond the surface of an apparently idyllic rural existence soon emerges. It is therefore not surprising that Kennelly recalls writing out by hand Kavanagh's excoriating 1942 epic *The Great Hunger* in the National Library in Dublin when a student in Trinity College in the 1950s, an early indication of his fondness for Irish interpretations of the epic form.

Today, the family pub is still situated on a corner of the crossroads and is run by Alan, one of his brothers. Like many small pubs in Kerry, the walls are adorned with black and white photographs of All-Ireland winning Gaelic football teams which, as well as members of Kennelly's own family, include the poet himself back in the Kerry minor team of 1954. Kennelly's first of two novels, *The Crooked Cross*, published in 1963, derives its title from the geographical layout of his home village and it is a novel that gives an early indication of the dominant concerns that would feature in his later and better-known poetry. The novel typically eschews an idealised portrayal of Irish village life in favour of a complex exploration of the devastating effects of emigration in rural Ireland, symbolically represented by the unusually severe drought affecting the village at the time. In his brief but insightful essay on this and *The Florentines*, Kennelly's second novel published in 1967, Terence Brown appositely notes Kennelly's "early suspicion of mere chronology" in texts characterised by "lyric intensity, symbolism, imagistic juxtaposition and epic directness of style" (Pine, 1994: 57), key foundational principles to be seen at work in nearly all of his later poetry.

At the age of twelve, after his primary education in the local school, Kennelly was sent to a school in nearby Tarbert run by Jane Agnes McKenna, to whom the 1992 collection *Breathing Spaces* is dedicated. She had started her own private secondary school for local children with a fee of three pounds a term. Kennelly's esteem for the high quality of education which he received in Tarbert is well known and he recalls many positive elements of this period of his childhood and education throughout his poetry. In 1952, Kennelly obtained a scholarship to attend Trinity College in Dublin and at the age of twenty-five he was awarded a joint first-class honours degree in French and English. It was in Trinity that he met Rudi Holzapfel with whom he was to jointly publish his first four books of poetry between 1959 and 1963. Kennelly was certainly not the typical Trinity student of the 1950s in that he was from a rural, Catholic background which contrasted sharply with the remnants of the Anglo-Irish Protestant ascendancy who populated the corridors of Trinity. Holzapfel, who now runs a bookshop in Cashel, County Tipperary notes:

> We must have been the two oddest denizens of Trinity at that time. He was like the proverbial culchie — he had a belted mac, a little cap down over his eyes and a little suitcase that he carried around with him. (McDonagh, 1990)

In 1959, Kennelly and Holzapfel published a collection of their poems entitled *Cast a Cold Eye*, of which 250 copies were sold along with a reprint of 100. With the publication of *Green Townlands* in 1963, their brief but fertile poetic collaboration came to an end and Kennelly returned to Dublin from Leeds, where he had been studying under Professor A. Norman Jeffares, to complete his doctoral studies. His doctorate, awarded by Trinity College in 1966, indicates the gestation of his long-held fascination not only with the traditional epic form in Irish poetry but with its many contemporary manifestations. Entitled *Modern Irish Poets and the Irish Epic*, the thesis traces the use of the epic style by various "modern" Irish poets, from the early work of Sir Samuel Ferguson and Aubrey De Vere to the more modernist interpretations of W.B. Yeats, George Russell and Austin Clarke. It is clear from this early work that the epic form is going to play a key role in the development of Kennelly's poetic *oeuvre*. From then his academic career steadily advanced from junior to senior lecturer in the Department of English at the University and he has been Professor of Modern Literature at Trinity College since 1973. Declan Kiberd recalls his undergraduate days in Kennelly's lectures in which Kennelly "praised Keats, according to my notes, for putting common place snatches of talk into his poems" (Persson, 1996: 81), a stylistic characteristic that was to feature large in his later poetic epic sequences.

Kennelly's poetic output is impressive by any standard. Since he published his first solo collection of poems *Let Fall No Burning Leaf* in 1963, over forty books of poetry have appeared in print, currently culminating with his 2003 collection, *Martial Art*. Although he is known principally as a poet, one of the hallmarks of Kennelly's eclectic body of work is his willingness to explore a wide variety of genres, like Heaney, from translations of ancient and medieval Irish poetic texts to versions of Euripides' *Medea* and Sophocles' *Antigone*, which have been performed to critical acclaim in Dublin and abroad. He is also a perceptive and insightful critic, something he also shares with Heaney, a fact attested to by the brilliant essays contained in Åke Persson's 1994 collection of his prose entitled *Journey into Joy*. These essays provide critical insights into Kennelly's personal literary tastes and display an easy command of a breadth of classical and contemporary literature and also point to the key formative influences on the development of his work. The essays include "A View of Irish Poetry", first published in 1970, in which Kennelly clearly enunciates the key developmental moments in Irish poetry. Significantly, the essay is divided into a pre- and post-Yeatsian poetic environment, with the latter characterised by Kennelly's wish for poetry to be "adventurous, daring, even offensive" (Kennelly, 1994: 57).

One of the recurring features of these writings is Kennelly's liking for a clear and uncluttered criticism and a preference for texts that challenge whatever socio-cultural *status quo* within which they find themselves operating. This consistent feature of both his creative and critical work, therefore, suggests an edgy intellect unwilling to allow ideas or concepts to rest easily on their perceived foundations, as well as a liking for poets who challenge the dominant ideologies of their time. Throughout his work, Kennelly challenges foundational human principles on a huge scale, stubbornly resisting both tradition and modernity in the same breath, finding a bruised and confused humanity in the midst of the chaos. Indeed, the idea of a book like this would, in many ways, be anathema to Kennelly as he has, as Kiberd has noted, consistently resisted politicisations of his work. He has also edited numerous books, including a selection of Irish drama, the works of Jonathan Swift and the poetry of James Joyce. He has been, since 1970, the editor of *The Penguin Book of Irish Verse*, an important and influential responsibility given that book's recurrent popularity. In the introduction, Kennelly identifies a key characteristic of Irish poetry:

> If I had to generalise about all Irish poetry and say what single quality strikes me most from *The Deer's Cry*, attributed to St Patrick, to *The Great Hunger* by Patrick Kavanagh, I would say that a hard, simple, virile, rhetorical clarity is its most memorable characteristic. (Kennelly, 1970: 27)

When writing this introductory note, Kennelly was in fact also outlining one of the major characteristics of his own poetry, namely the drive for exactness of observation. Using religious metaphors in one of his early poems, "The Blind Man", he describes his poetic drive as the search for light in a darkness that envelops him like a "velvet kingdom" (*CO*, 34). This darkness is presented by Kennelly as neither evil nor sinister but rather as an obscuring force that the poet must overcome through a passionate exposing of the faint apparitions of a barely perceptible light. He does this by close observation of his subject and he presents his own poetic abilities, with characteristic modesty, as those of the blind man prodding his way through life not merely as a result of a natural instinct but armed with a dogged determination to survive. The paradoxical and juxtaposed relationship between tragedy and comedy throughout Kennelly's work is mirrored by his description of the poetic exercise as the exploration of the contradictions of light and darkness, hope and despair and the tentative unravelling of these contradictions and their manifestation in various aspects of life. He concludes his poem with an admission of the inherent weakness of the poetic exercise when he outlines that he is "conscious of the things I'm fit to share, acknowledging the light I've been denied" (*CO*, 35). This reversal of the conventional poetic metaphor of the journey towards illumination is echoed by Seamus Heaney in the opening line of his poem, "The Forge", in which he writes that "All I know is a door into the dark" (Heaney, 1969: 19), an image which lends itself to the title of his fourth collection, *Door Into The Dark*, published in 1969. Both poets appear to eschew the traditional imagery of light and dark in favour of a more modest and humble acknowledgement of their respective poetic missions. This early questioning of the efficacy of poetry itself becomes an increasingly important question raised by Kennelly as his poetry develops and his gradual fondness for the epigram, noticeable in 1999's *Begin* and emerging as the central motif of 2003's *Martial Art*, indicates a distrust of the potential meanderings of the long poem in favour of the tart succinctness of the shorter form.

Generally, it can be said that the rhythm of Kennelly's poetry appears paramount, with other aspects of the poetic exercise subordinate to the literal "flow" of a poem. His first collection, entitled *Getting Up Early* (1966), gives numerous examples of the variety of rhyming schemes and metrical structures, from a standard Petrarchan sonnet concerning a pair of old men to the subtle rhyme of "The Gift", whose form subtly acts as an undercurrent to the content of the poem. In fact, when Kennelly describes his ability to compose poetry as "a gift that took me unawares" (*CO*, 1) it could equally be argued that Kennelly's poetry illustrates a close attention to both form and style in the production of effective, contained and independent poems. The popular image of the untutored genius does not accurately apply to Kennelly and his ability to compose in a variety of regular rhythmical styles indicates a poet who is fascinated by form. This is attested to by Rudi Holzapfel who has noted:

> What did unify us was, funnily enough, a belief in rhyme and metre, and a belief in something which the old Gaelic poets believed in. They were very adamant about the form of a poem. (McDonagh, 1990)

The themes explored by Kennelly in his poetry are as varied as the metrical and rhythmical patterns employed therein. The celebration and concurrent demythologisation of rural life characterises many of his early collections and are a strong element of the 1992 collection of early poetry entitled *Breathing Spaces*. He explores the apparent contradictions inherent in the natural world where survival is the lowest common denominator and extreme violence the *modus operandi* of both animals and humans. The impression of nature that the reader gleans from such poems as "Mastery", "The Pig-killer", and "Time for the Knife" is one of cynical human manipulation of the natural world where the value of a non-human life is judged purely in terms of its economic or social value. The brutality of animal slaughter in farmyard sheds and outhouses, performed with clinical precision and a casual nonchalance born out of repetition, is observed by Kennelly in a cool and detailed manner that is neither judgemental nor sentimental but rather detached, allowing the reader to enter into a poem that appears open-ended, taking from it whatever impressions it makes on the mind. It is in these poems of nature, violence and survival that Kennelly's skill as an apparently detached recorder of detail emerges and it is through these poems, characterised by what Gerald Dawe refers to as the "unforced, indifferent mystery" (Pine, 1994: 61) of subtle presentation, that Kennelly captures the "essence" of a particular situation.

In "That Look", for example, Kennelly describes the killing of a rat by a wire-haired terrier in a farmyard and the poem is full of a "throaty menace hard and full" (*ATFV*, 55) which fills the space between the rat and the dog. Kennelly highlights the fear that characterises the overt tranquillity of the natural world and firmly establishes humans as the unassailable masters of the hierarchy of survival. The rat is terrified of the terrier, which is in turn terrified by Scanlon, who ultimately holds the balance of life and death in his hands. With the signal given by Scanlon, the terrier strikes:

> The terrier killed the fear and hate in
> The rat's eyes. I've seen that look in people's faces.

By linking the "fear and hate" in the rat's eyes to his experience of people, Kennelly places human emotions, and our perceptions of them, in the same category as the raw emotions experienced by animals in situations of life and death. Feelings of love, hate, desire and jealousy, for example, are often subordinated to a sense of ethics or rationality, and the dialogic nature of many of Kennelly's poems can be viewed as a hermeneutical tool used to tease out the multiplicity of responses to any given situation. This poem points to the complex nature of our emotions and the extent to which deep instinctual forces can be repressed, or at least controlled, by our conscious mind. The collection *Dream of a Black Fox*, published in 1968, highlights the poet's recurring interests which he outlined in the introduction to his *Selected Poems* of 1969:

> They [his poems] are deliberate repetition of a few
> things I have always found interesting: the attempt to
> understand the nature of good and evil; the essence of
> contradiction; the relationships of forces such as cruelty
> and corruption to the human passion and need for sur-
> vival; they desirability of continuing, of waking up again
> and walking out into the morning light. (*SP*, 1969: *xii*)

This last point is of great significance when considering the
poetry of Brendan Kennelly. The elitist myth surrounding the
act of poetic creation is dealt a fatal blow in much of Ken-
nelly's work. Far from engaging in some form of self-
aggrandisement through an obscure and self-absorbed set of
poetic symbols, Kennelly's poetry emerges from "the byways,
laneways, backyards, nooks and crannies of self" in which he
engages in an almost self-destructive dialogue with his many
competing psyches. He also manages to avoid a false self-
deprecation in which the poet is depicted as the mere recep-
tacle of a muse-inspired, collective wisdom, devoid of personal
control or experience. His skill as a poet lies in his acute per-
ception of the boundary between self and poem, a tentative
balance that requires concentration and vigilance to maintain.

In "The Gift", significantly the opening poem in one of his
most popular and important selections, *A Time for Voices*, he
acknowledges the fragile and wonderfully ordinary nature of
the poetic exercise:

> It came slowly.
> Afraid of insufficient self-content
> Or some inherent weakness in itself
> Small and hesitant
> Like children at the tops of stairs
> It came through shops, rooms, temples,
>
> Streets, places that were badly lit.
> It was a gift that took me unawares
> And I accepted it. (*ATFV*, 15)

Brendan Kennelly is a poet who cherishes clarity and constantly seeks to avoid the deadening effect of presenting an artificially balanced view of life through his poetry. By operating at the extremities of form, theme and chronology, he attempts to speak to the centre by expressing the margins.

He acknowledges a disparate international range of poetic influences, from, amongst others, Rimbaud, Kavanagh, Baudelaire and Ginsberg and their influence finds threads of expression throughout his work (Murphy, 1987: 50). While the debt to Kavanagh has long been recognised, not only by Kennelly but by many contemporary Irish poets, the influence of the others is certainly palpable in the body of Kennelly's work. It is interesting to note that Rimbaud, Baudelaire and Ginsberg each challenged the social and cultural norms of their respective eras and as a result faced both social opprobrium and literary censorship. Each adopted what could be termed a counter-cultural perspective in their poetry, focusing on the marginalised and dispossessed in dark, disturbing but often frequently hilarious verse. It is undoubtedly the searing socio-cultural critique offered in the work of these poets that attracted Kennelly, and their utilisation of a variety of forms, combining traditional and modern influences, would alert an aspiring poet to the effectiveness of a multiplicity of techniques. Interestingly, in an essay on the poetry of Derek Mahon, Kennelly refers to "other writers who appear as helpers" in the construction of Mahon's poetic universe, writers who act as a "kind of private army of conscience", operating as "an aid toward self scrutiny and self revelation" (Kennelly, 1994: 135). Among these writers is Arthur Rimbaud, and it certainly can be argued that he, along with Ginsberg, Kavanagh and Baudelaire, features strongly in Kennelly's personal poetic soldiers of fortune.

Kennelly is, in many ways, an apparent contradiction in that he has risen to the top of the academic world in Ireland, eschewing the inevitable political machinations while maintaining close links with his roots and the people he grew up

with. In *This Fellow with the Fabulous Smile*, edited by Åke Pers-
son and published by Bloodaxe Books in 1996, a series of Irish
public figures pay their personal tributes to Kennelly and the
book abounds with stories of personal generosity, ribald noc-
turnal adventures and references to Kennelly's famous facial
dimples. The book occasionally teeters on the verge of carica-
ture in which the myth of the man overshadows the power
and crucial cultural significance of his work and the title goes a
long way to explaining a good deal of the popular perception of
both Kennelly and his work. It is perhaps this perceived acces-
sibility that has shied critics away from his work, while more
"difficult" poets such as Medbh McGuckian and Eavan Boland
attract a good deal of critical attention. Kennelly's role in the
development of contemporary Irish poetry is often unfairly
confined to the margins of the larger texts of Heaney, Mul-
doon and Montague, despite the fact that books such as
Cromwell and *The Book of Judas* are seminal texts in the emer-
gence of one of the most important counter-critical voices in
contemporary Irish literature. Indeed, in an essay in *Dark
Fathers Into Light*, Gus Martin, on more than one occasion, re-
fers to Kennelly as "recklessly prolific" and, in a classic moment
of critical self-aggrandisement, he comments that "the user
friendly popularity of the poetry itself may have constituted a
mixed blessing for his reputation" (Pine, 1994: 36). The strange
juxtaposition of popularity and critical opprobrium clearly
places the role of the critic in the establishment of a poetic
reputation at a higher status than that of the public response to
the poetry itself, especially in terms of what Martin refers to as
the "first restless decade" of Kennelly's work.

Perhaps this is one of the reasons why he is concerned, in
his poetry, with the nature of contradictions, such as the ex-
istence of violence in what appears natural and the narrow-
ness of the boundary between good and evil. His major
concern is the pursuit of honesty and clarity and he lives his
life with the freedom afforded to him by his healthy disre-

spect for convention. His popularity in Ireland is based on his personal accessibility and on his ability to reflect on life with candour, insight and humour. However, this book will seek to show that on closer examination, the poetry of Brendan Kennelly can be perceived as a dangerous, challenging and tautly constructed body of work that offers a searing social and cultural critique. His principal source of inspiration is the everyday conversation of people going about the process of coping with life and much of his poetry reflects what could be termed the wisdom born out of survival. Kennelly comments:

> One of my favourite pastimes is reading the *Oxford English Dictionary*, and I'll take a word and trace its joyous history. It reminds me of my own life, and struggle of a work to survive its own stages, to stay alive, to serve a young boy or girl who's encountering that word for the first time, and behind it are centuries of experience, and it's in the mouth of that child, and that's joy to me, the word as a survivor. (Pine, 1990)

The intention of this book is to concentrate on a selection of Kennelly's texts which will act as exemplars of the major thematic concerns that have driven his work over the years. Consequently, this process will inevitably involve the elision of certain collections in favour of the better-known material. Chapter One will focus on Kennelly's early poetry, a period beginning with his early collaborations with Rudi Holzapfel in the late 1950s up to the publication of *The Boats Are Home* in 1980. This is a period of intense activity for Kennelly, where the genesis of his fascination with concepts such as betrayal, violence and passionate love are clearly seen. His early poetry, however, should not merely be seen in the light of his better-known later work, as it includes some incredibly assured work in its own right and there are many interesting examples of Kennelly experimenting with a variety of forms and themes. His *Selected Poems* of 1969 is a highly confident collection and there is certainly a case to be made that it represents as good a collection as the better-known *A Time for Voices*, published in 1990.

Chapter Two will look specifically at the importance of the themes of education and childhood in the development of Kennelly's oeuvre, tightly collected in *The Boats Are Home*, published in 1980. These poems take a dark look at the consequences of the casual brutality that characterised many aspects of Kennelly's upbringing but also point to that search for meaning and form in spite of the violence. Chapter Three is devoted almost entirely to *Cromwell*, arguably Kennelly's most important long poem and certainly one of his best known. Published in 1983, the poem marks a watershed in his utilisation of the dialogic interchange between a variety of characters, principal amongst whom is Buffun, the troubled protagonist, whose exchanges with a time-travelling Oliver Cromwell shed crucial hermeneutical light on conflicting concepts of Irish identity, language, history and religion.

Chapter Four concentrates on Kennelly's powerful 1991 version of Euripides' *Medea*, one of four "versions" of plays written by Kennelly. Medea's justifications for her infamous infanticide drive the play into controversial and troubling territory and Kennelly's version focuses on the nature of Medea's anger, manifested in the most unnatural of crimes. Chapter Five places 1996's *The Book of Judas* in the forefront of Kennelly's canon of work, extending and developing the themes previously explored in Cromwell. The social and cultural ubiquity of betrayal in Ireland drives this epic collection and the contextualising of the poems allows Kennelly to explore the ambiguous and confused relationship between the historical Jesus and his contemporary manifestations. The concluding chapter will examine Kennelly's brilliantly expressed concept of "Blitzophrenia" as the defining characteristic of his long and varied career.

Chapter One

Getting Up Early

Brendan Kennelly's first selected poems, entitled *Collection One: Getting Up Early*, was published by Allen Figgis and Co. Ltd. in Dublin in 1966, and it is an early indication of the eclectic influences and genres that were to characterise his later and better-known work. It is an extraordinarily assured collection, ranging from poems questioning the very nature of the poetic exercise to the Moloney mini-epics that had first appeared a year previously in *Up and At It*. The often ambiguous influence of Kennelly's north Kerry heritage predominates, from lingering metaphors of the Shannon river to the haunting presence of pre-Christian sites such as Lislaughtin Abbey. An analysis of this early poetry provides some important contexts for the epic works to follow. The collection moves easily from complex and allegorical poems like "My Dark Fathers" to the picaresque adventures of Moloney, and strong connections can be traced between this collection and the more recent *Begin* (1999), with both collections contrasting long narrative poems with an almost epigrammatic insight into the vagaries of human nature. The poems are an early indication of the ambiguous relationship between Kennelly and his birthplace, a relationship suffused with warmth and yet tinged with a palpable distance and yearning for escape. This provides the collection with an edginess that is a central feature of much of

Kennelly's early work, and in the figure of Johnny Gobless, a ubiquitous village idiot, the ideology of a man who "hounded truth until it cried" (*CO*, 31) foreshadows that troubled protagonist Buffun, a man whose encounters with his personal demons lead him to conclude that his mind is "a mirror for a dimwit" (*C*, 114). These two figures personify the liminal space between perceived sanity and madness that Kennelly has so successfully explored throughout his work.

The collection includes what for many poetry anthologists has become Kennelly's signature poem, "My Dark Fathers", and the final stanza indicates the fascination with the outsider that was to characterise his later epic collections:

> Since I am of Kerry clay and rock,
> I celebrate the darkness and the shame
> That could compel a man to turn his face
> Against the wall, withdrawn from light so strong
> And undeceiving, spancelled in a place
> Of unapplauding hands and broken song. (*CO*, 29)

This uncompromising image of a man reduced to the status of a tethered animal evokes strong connections with Patrick Maguire, Patrick Kavanagh's great rural anti-hero. Equally, Kennelly's north Kerry "clay and rock" echoes the "stony grey soil" of Kavanagh's Monaghan (Kavanagh, 1972: 73), both poets evoking images of a cloying, muddy environment in which all hope of personal pleasure and escape are subsumed under the weight of a closed community. When Kennelly empathises with the "darkness and the shame" of his Kerry homeland, Patrick Maguire, in the final section of *The Great Hunger*, is faced with a parallel silent ironic applause as the final curtain comes down on his futile existence. Indeed, the very images of light and song that Kennelly evokes in "My Dark Fathers" are strongly paralleled in Maguire's imaginary epitaph:

He will hardly remember that life happened to him —
Something was brighter a moment. Somebody sang in the
   distance. (Kavanagh, 1984: 103)

The decade of the 1960s set Kennelly in the company of
other emerging and established poetic voices, including Sea-
mus Heaney, John Montague, Thomas Kinsella and Richard
Murphy, and it is perhaps the emergence of such distinct
voices that has led to the elision of critical responses to Ken-
nelly's early work and the somewhat unfair accusation of
reckless prolificacy. Indeed, excluding the co-authored works
with Rudi Holzapfel and collections of previously published
poems, Kennelly published four books of poetry in the period
1959 to 1970, hardly a case of over-production. Equally, these
poems clearly indicate the emergence of a distinct and robust
poetic voice, refreshingly free from the derivative influences
that usually retrospectively characterise the emergence of a
major new poetic voice.

"My Dark Fathers" concerns itself intently with the brutal-
ity, depression and monotony of Irish rural life, themes that
dominate subsequent collections like *Dream of a Black Fox*
(1968) and *Salvation: The Stranger* (1972) and his desire to shed
light on the darker sides of Irish public and private life is pal-
pable. The eponymous title poem is a visceral debunking of
rural mythology, peopled by figures living "the intolerable day"
in an environment bordered by "the encroaching sea", blend-
ing disturbing and ambiguous images of a crucified couple with
a grey and inhospitable countryside. In the introduction to his
1969 *Selected Poems*, Kennelly gives an extended contextuali-
sation of the poem, noting that it was an attempt "to define
my own relationship with Irish history" (*SP*, 1969: *xii*), and this
relationship certainly went on to be one of the dominating
factors in the development of his poetry. Although the poem
is based around details given by Frank O'Connor in a talk
about the Famine, the contemporary social and cultural paral-

lels drive the poem's critique of what Kennelly refers to as "the modern middle-class commitment to complacency and swinish apathy".

Later, in the introduction to his 1990 selection *A Time For Voices*, Kennelly refers to "My Dark Fathers" as a conscious attempt to portray the past as a "savage educator, capable of defining the present with brutal precision" (*ATFV*, 11), and this image of the repetitive cycle of history bearing down on contemporary existence establishes one of Kennelly's main poetic concerns. The poem portrays a past that casts a long shadow over the present, and it can certainly be argued that this long historical shadow is given a close analysis in Kennelly's later epic sequences.

The collection also highlights many of Kennelly's major poetic strengths, particularly his ability to focus on the minute details of quotidian rural events: everything from animal slaughtering to hedge trimming, and, through the use of spare imagery and concrete language, imbue these actions with a perpetual significance in which the essence of a community strives towards an unpretentious and unselfconscious definition. "The Pig-Killer", for example, another well-anthologised poem, is one of many poems that Augustine Martin refers to as "curt, seminal images of rural life" (Pine, 1994: 49), and it portrays a rurality strongly reminiscent of Kavanagh's *The Great Hunger* and presaging Seamus Heaney's *Death of a Naturalist*. The calm brutality of the men and the precise execution of the pig evokes a community low on sentiment and driven by bare economic needs with the environment, and all it contains, being merely a means towards survival rather than an aesthetic backdrop to some form of idyllic existence. Kennelly's early collections contain a good deal of poems which refer to killing of one sort or another, be it the blithe and unsentimental rural attitude to slaughter or the more spectacular but equally brutal killings that occur as part of a regular natural cycle.

There are also many fascinating connections to be made between Kennelly's early poetry and the later epic collections. It is clear from a poem like "At Table" from his 1967 collection *Good Souls to Survive* that Kennelly was experimenting with the dialogic form that was to be such a key feature of the success of both *Cromwell* and *The Book of Judas*. In the poem, the recurring Kennellian poetic motif of the table dominates, a constant presence in the shifting history of humanity. Tables frequently are used by Kennelly in his poetry, the images fluctuating from a scene of violent animal deaths to the precise and minute dissection of reputations and personalities at ostensibly polite dinner parties. The irony of the place of death doubling as the place of nourishment and the element of enforced sacrifice involved is certainly not lost on Kennelly, and this early subversion of the image of the table as the centre of familial discourse indicates that his poetry is constantly seeking to explore dominant social and cultural icons in terms of their ability to subvert the very values they purport to represent. (Indeed, in *Martial Art*, Martial learns a good deal of his assumptions about human nature while dining, largely ungratefully, at the tables of various friends and acquaintances.) In this context, the meeting of "Christ" and "Iscariot" (*GSTS*, 45) at the same table where, in verse one, the reputation of a writer is dissected over polite "sips of tea", is hugely significant. Judas is "a disgruntled man", partially embarrassed by the "flushed recognition reddening his face" and partly annoyed at Jesus' apparently calm and matter-of-fact acceptance of his upcoming betrayal, and in the fifth verse Kennelly asks the seminal question:

> Without the treacherous Iscariot
> Would man have Christ for an eternal friend? (*GSTS*, 46)

The image of the crucified Christ is then mirrored with the swaying body of the hung Judas, and the sacrifice of the latter is strongly portrayed as the decisive contributing factor in the "inevitable triumph" of the former. This poem, published twenty-four years before *The Book of Judas*, portrays a "sea" of betrayal, and the ritualised cannibalisation of a whale on "Cloghane Strand" merely enforces the dominant, bloody images of the "sea's fat gift" being brutally hacked to pieces by a man who "doesn't give a tinker's curse". Survival, and all the concomitant suffering and victimisation that entails, is portrayed as the driving force behind much human behaviour, and one of the strongest features of the later *Book of Judas* is the eponymous hero's recognition of his simple desire to survive the opprobrium that history has heaped upon him.

This image of blushing embarrassment in "At Table" is repeated in "Let Me Be The Thing I Am" from *The Book of Judas* when Judas requests that "if you see my face blush till the blood is fit to break the skin", judgement must be suspended because, after all, Judas is the fabrication of the contemporary mind and therefore his blushing makes "my lie your truth, my truth your lie" (*J*, 279). The close intellectual, imagistic and emotional interweaving of what are popularly held to be polar opposites features strongly throughout Kennelly's work, a juxtaposition most illuminatingly illustrated by his constant referral to Jesus and Judas, one of the iconic relationships in the Judeo-Christian tradition. In many ways, this recurring, troubled dialogue finds its most peaceful resolution in Kennelly's 1998 poem *The Man Made of Rain*, when the multifarious manifestations that have populated his poetry from its inception find their true home in the shape of the watery phantasm that gently leads the poet down familiar if sometimes unrecognised roads.

In *Up and At It*, first published in 1965 and reprinted as *Moloney Up and At It* in 1984, close attention to rhythm, metre and rhyme realistically captures the oral tradition that was clearly a huge influence in the development of Kennelly's noted rhythmical fluency. Based around the reflections of the central character of Moloney, these comic poems concern the picaresque stories and anecdotes that were a central feature in the mythology of any rural village. Written in the vernacular, the six poems in this collection highlight Kennelly's mastery not only of the obsessions of his native people but also of the importance of form to the successful and entertaining completion of a story. The Moloney series of poems revolves around the life, reflections and dreams of Moloney, who recounts his stories of death and sex in the quick and easy manner of the practised storyteller, and this collection highlights Kennelly's comic skill, an important element in much of his poetry.

The poems are written in the first person singular, a method which Kennelly describes as a "great distancer" which allows him to immerse himself in Moloney and thereby write from within the freedom of another "voice", a voice which reflects the wisdom and humour of the oral tradition that he grew up with. The poems are written in the language of north Kerry where the emphasis on the traditional art of storytelling lies in the power and accuracy of observation and the fluency of presentation. Each poem is recounted by Moloney to some imaginary audience and the topics revolve around the major interests and preoccupations of the local people, namely drink, sex, love, religion and death. Moloney is an "Everyman" figure who has his own theology and philosophy of life based, not on theory, but on the rather more subjective and personal plane of experience. Whatever wisdom he possesses has been gleaned from observing the world as it appears to him. In the title poem, for example, on the night of his mother's funeral, Moloney meets a woman in a pub and after an evening of drinking and talking they end up having sex in the graveyard of the local church. In the middle of this he realises that they are actually lying on top of his mother's freshly dug grave, but he does not allow this Freudian situation to upset him:

"Yerra, you might
As well enjoy the gift o' the night
While you have the chance", I said
To myself, realizin' the dead are dead,
Past holiness and harms —
And the living' woman in my arms. (*MUAI*, 12)

Moloney typifies the hope that is to be found in much of Kennelly's poetry. Moloney's philosophy is based on the realisation that life is relatively short and should be lived to its fullest potential and passion, and this is exactly what he attempts to do. The collection also highlights Kennelly's comic touch in that the situations that Moloney finds himself in vary from the unusual to the improbable, and all are told with close attention to the rhyming structures and rhythmical patterns indispensable in effective comic poetry. The real comedy to be found in Moloney is in the quirks and habits of the people who share his life and their largely positive attitudes towards life, death and survival. Kennelly has long insisted that essentially he has come from an oral poetic tradition and that his poetry is best appreciated when all the inflections, accents and rhythms of spoken poetry are taken into account. These poems highlight Kennelly's fervent belief in the vitality of life and of the necessity of approaching every event in life with a sense of hope. This hope does not spring from a naïve faith that somehow circumstances will improve but rather from the more prosaic concept of dogged determination.

Indeed, it is interesting to note the similarities between Moloney's adventures in North Kerry and the perambulations of Martial in Kennelly's latest collection *Martial Art*. The protagonists are separated by two millennia but share the same delight in picking up whatever wisdom they can from a variety of often risqué and precarious situations. Their apparent openness, however, masks a canny perceptiveness that they both use to their advantage, as Martial notes:

If Martial's truth were told
All that I give
Would be less than I withhold. (*MA*, 50)

In the canon of Kennelly's pre-*Cromwell* poetry, *Shelley in Dublin*, first published 1974, stands out as a key developmental moment, in that it contains his first sustained long narrative poem, a device he was to develop and adapt to such effect over the rest of his career. The poem covers the various incidents and episodes experienced by Percy Bysshe Shelley during his brief two-month stay in Ireland in 1812, ten years before his death in 1822, and the poem marks a watershed in the complex progression of Kennelly's technique. In *Dream of a Black Fox*, for instance, published in 1968, Kennelly flirts with the narrative poem, peppering the collection with strange allegorical journeys in which the first-person poet engages with largely sinister and threatening figures who lead him, Pilgrim-like, towards a hesitant, unsettling and often unstable image of self. The poem "Nightmare" typifies this early experimentation, in which sleep is compared to a "black pit" (*DBF*, 61), an image that finds a strong echo twenty-five years later in *Cromwell* with Buffun's description of his nocturnal world: "Night. The pits are everywhere" (*C*, 16). *Shelley in Dublin* develops this technique further, blending the surreal elements of his early narrative poems with the detail of a recorded, documented episode in history, an amalgamation that provides the narrative with a credible and preordained structure that was to prove so successful in his later epic sequences.

The accuracy of the narrative, based as it is on a visit to Ireland by Shelley that was contemporaneously recorded, is central to the effectiveness of Kennelly's poem, and he bases his narrative on Shelley's published pamphlets, poems and letters, a series of letters from Shelley's wife Harriet and Richard Holmes's 1974 biography *Shelley: The Pursuit*. The poem traces Shelley's sincere but ineffectual desire to initiate change in Ireland, cleverly adopting both a third and first person narrative voice, blurring the perspectives within the poem in order to destabilise the reader and to allow Kennelly to move freely in and out of history, touching the past when relevant and then imperceptibly shifting into the contemporary, and it is clear that in *Shelley in Dublin* he is developing and maturing a poetic hermeneutic and style which would be a predominant feature of his later work. Shelley's concerns, expressed through a variety of speeches and letters strikingly parallel Kennelly's poetic manifesto as expressed in the preface to *The Book of Judas*, both expressing the need to confront polite social and cultural apathy and a stultifying personal ineffectualness. Shelley's initial zeal, prompted as it was out of a genuine concern for the state of Ireland in the early nineteenth century, soon gives way to a seething anger at what he perceives to be a self-serving political elite:

> And all the others
> Those who talk so much
> Who are they?
> Thumping in and out, spewing anecdotes,
> Full of plans and schemes,
> Good-natured, drunk,
> Doing nothing. (*SID*, 11)

Similarly, in the preface to *The Book of Judas*, Kennelly warns against a "half-heartedness" that he sees eating away at the core of personal and national identity, and it is a statement that could equally apply to the post-Celtic Tiger state of the Irish nation:

> We have made ourselves into half-people. Half-heartedness is a slow, banal killer. It is also, paradoxically, a creepy pathway towards "success", especially if the half-heartedness is of the polished variety. (*J*, 11)

Shelley's desire for change is portrayed by Kennelly as a genuine human concern for those perceived to be in a subaltern position. Dublin in 1812 appears as a stultified exemplar of chronic social division, a city that "had known only tyranny for centuries" (*SID*, 5) and one which is peopled by the "beaten dead" (*SID*, 10). The poverty, filth and apathy of the citizens of the city appears beyond redemption and Shelley quickly loses faith not only in the citizens of Dublin but also in his ability to rouse them out of their perceived stupor. His address, delivered with such passion and belief, is cleverly manipulated by Kennelly in that he tampers with the original account of the speech by adding phrases of his own, a methodology he was to employ with increased effectiveness in his versions of *Medea*, *The Trojan Women* and *Antigone* in the 1990s. This device is hugely effective across the broad spectrum of Kennelly's poetry and drama in that it allows him a good deal of hermeneutical freedom to explore and express what he perceives to be the genuine emotional foundations underpinning human actions and words.

Shelley's ordinariness emerges through Kennelly's intrusions, the somewhat idealistic rhetoric of his *Address*, peppered with frustrated asides as well as the impatience of the idealist faced with the intransigence of the political system. Shelley's rapidly flagging enthusiasm for the redemption of the Irish people is portrayed as the response of a genuinely sympathetic soul being overwhelmed by the complex sociopolitical currents which swamp his every move. Again, this is a recurring theme in Kennelly's work and in nearly every collection there are poems resisting what he refers to as "that sluggishness that wants to seduce/ambush us all into upright, respectable, 'mature' competent corpses" (*ATFV*, 12). It is also telling that in the note to *Shelley in Dublin*, Kennelly quotes at some length a passage from Jean Overton Fuller's biography of Shelley that refers to the latter's passionate belief in the concept of the Illuminees: "a nucleus of illuminated souls which . . .

would achieve such a magnification of their lights together as should constitute a sun" (*SP*, 1985: 118). In this context, it can certainly be argued that the subjects of Kennelly's epic sequences constitute a hugely influential nucleus in the development of popular perceptions of the concept of Irish identity, from the aesthetic and the religious to the political.

The style of *Shelley in Dublin* certainly indicates that Kennelly is very much at home in his unique reworking of the epic genre. In a collection entitled in *The House That Jack Didn't Build* published in 1982 by the same small Dublin-based Beaver Row Press who were to publish *Cromwell* the following year, he appears to be scouting the ground that will become the scene of the full-scale battle that is *Cromwell*. Juxtaposing the conflicting concerns of the coloniser and the colonised in the guise of the confident, voracious Jack and the "skulking" former tenant in "The Statement of the Former Occupant", the former occupant of an anonymous house occupied by a character called Jack is reluctantly forced to admit that Jack has made the rooms of his former home "more elegant than I can say" (*HJDB*, 14) while still vowing to remove Jack by force if necessary. He dreams of a day when he can free himself "from my stinking pit to savour your exquisite order" (*HJDB*, 14) although the former occupant is, consequently, a source of massive contradiction, bitterly resenting his expulsion yet admiring the changes wrought upon his property by the new occupier. This mirrors many of the inherent problems associated with the early years of the Irish Free State in which the new government sought to distance itself from the political and cultural influence of the coloniser, while maintaining, virtually intact, the colonial forms of education, judiciary and civil service.

Any acknowledgement of the benefits of the colonial period would possibly have shattered the fragile image of nationhood in the immediate postcolonial era, composed as it was in a climate of opposition and civil war, an identity formed in adversity and opposition. Much of Kennelly's epic poetry can be regarded, therefore, as an attempted expression of the complexities surrounding the definition of personal and national identity. He articulates those he regards as voiceless and analyses the underlying and shifting influences that compose models of self and nation. He explores contradictions and seeks points of connection and intersection by posing more questions than seeking definitive answers and the adoption of real, historical personae in his later sequences adds a historical frisson to the general theories expounded in *The House That Jack Didn't Build*. It is clear, therefore, that in much of Kennelly's pre-*Cromwell* poetry there are discernable themes and methodologies that point to the genesis of his firmly held belief that "the poem is the arena where these voices engage each other in open and hidden combat, and continue to do so until they are heard" (*ATFV*, 12).

Chapter Two

Old Loyalties: *The Boats Are Home*

"I think what you're saying is that there are dominant images in any person's life and that you can spend the rest of your life unravelling the fears, terrors, hopes and loves that dominated your childhood up to the age of probably ten. There's an awful lot to be said for that, and to that extent I would return to my village, my parents, by brothers, my sisters, the sight of men getting drunk in a pub, tinkers beating the daylights out of each other, a son whipping his father."
(Pine, 1990: 21)

It is principally in his collection *The Boats Are Home*, published in 1980, that Kennelly portrays the "dominant images" of his childhood and early education. Given the centrality of both in the development of Kennelly's work, this collection plays a crucial and often overlooked role in his canon. In this compilation, containing some previously published works, Kennelly portrays seminal childhood events as tangible memories full of fear, despair, violence and humour. There are few of the cosy pastoral scenes one might expect from a poet growing up in a rural part of Ireland in the 1940s; instead the poems deal with a harsher existence, a quotidian mundanity punctuated by rare moments of light relief. The poems range over a broad spectrum of rural life, including education, religion,

violence, singing and rituals associated with death. To Ken-
nelly, memories become like "old loyalties" (Pine, 1990: 22)
that are not buried in the psyche but exist as tenable, tangible
and reconstructed realities in the present. The function of
Kennelly's poetry is not necessarily to deconstruct these
memories but to assimilate these often phantasmagorical im-
ages of childhood into contemporary perceptions of the
world and to tentatively position these images in the haphaz-
ard formation of the self. Indeed, this poetic methodology is
developed further in *The Man Made of Rain* when Kennelly is
taken on a journey that leads to his desire "to see the dream
absorb and transfigure its own violation by the 'real'" (*MMR*,
8–9), thus presaging the recollection of memories over what-
ever is perceived to be real in the present. This absorption,
re-evaluation and re-appropriation of memories and images
from the past into the present, rather than a mawkish self-
serving nostalgia, drives *The Boats Are Home* and indeed this
could be seen as a key driving force behind most of Ken-
nelly's epic work. This collection presents Kennelly as an oc-
casionally detached yet sensitive and emotional observer,
capable of standing back and recording the detail that forms
the essence of the captured moment his poem describes. In
language that echoes Heaney's "Digging", Kennelly has de-
scribed this complex inter-relationship between the memo-
rised past and the perceived present:

> "It's not a case of digging them up. It's not a process
> of disinterring. They revisit you. In a sense it's not the
> past as all. It's just images out of the past that happen
> to become living presence in your own life." (Carty,
> 1981: 16)

Kennelly peoples the poems with a mixture of real and
imagined individuals from his memories of Ballylongford and
what emerges is a powerful collection that is marked by a
hard-necked toleration of a difficult existence, marginally

more bearable than that of Francie Brady, anti-hero of Patrick McCabe's *The Butcher Boy*, but equally punctuated with moments of abject despair and manic levity. The book is clearly framed by images of youth and maturity, with the imagistic journey of the schoolboy buckling down to learn in the first poem "To Learn" completed by the bombastic, hypocritical and self-important anti-hero of "Six of One", the final poem in the collection. In much the same way that James Joyce's *Dubliners* can be perceived as marking the various rights of passage of a ubiquitous individual, it could therefore be argued that the poems in the collection chart the social and educational development of a single individual, from the insecure initial exposure to a harsh educational system to the diffracted, decentred and ultimately insecure blusterer that eventually emerges, and the influence of the former on the latter is clearly implied by the framing of the collection. Indeed, all of Kennelly's collections are marked by carefully constructed and selected introductory and concluding framing poems clearly designed to present each collection as a unified, progressive whole, and this is a key feature of *The Boats Are Home*. Far from portraying a romanticised view of a rural idyll Kennelly describes the key motivations of his early childhood society:

> "It was not a society that had set out to understand things. I remember very little understanding of anything. They understood that they had to cope with life. They understood that they had to make money. . . . All I remember is talking, trying to get on, lots of games, lots of football, lots of running." (Murphy, 1987: 48)

This is not to suggest the lives of the people of Ballylongford were mere economic drudgery but rather that the need to survive, provide a reasonable standard of living, and most crucially avoid emigration, occupied most of their time, and it can be clearly seen in Kennelly's 1999 collection *Begin*, for example, that this pragmatic utilitarianism, not usually associated with poetry, is a fundamental driving force behind much of Kennelly's work. Equally, in a collection entitled *Breathing Spaces*, published in 1992, Kennelly described his anthologised early poetry as being characterised by "themes that haunt me like obsessions", and many of these will be discussed in this analysis of *The Boats Are Home*. *Breathing Spaces* is an important book in that it includes reprints of significant works such as *Love Cry*, first published by Tara Telephone Publications in 1972, and *A Girl*, written in 1978 and an excellent early example of two of Kennelly's favoured poetic techniques: the adoption of a female voice and the extended poem sequence. In a nice and perhaps unintended irony, the cover of his 2001 collection *Glimpses* features Jan Vermeer's haunting portrait *Girl with a Pearl Earring*, an image that uncannily matches Kennelly description of the girl who inspired his earlier extended poem:

> I also recall the quick, dark way she had of throwing a glance over her shoulder as she moved away from you. A quick, shy glance, at once searching and furtive. She always seemed to be moving away into herself and always quickly scrutinising whoever she was leaving behind. (*BS*, 140)

The crucial role of storytelling and singing in the formation of a sense of communal identity is highlighted by Kennelly when he notes that "the people were always expressing themselves either in terms of a song or a story or an interest in character" (Murphy, 1987: 48) and this fascination with narrative and its regenerative capabilities echoes throughout Kennelly's work. "The Story", an important poem that captures the vital role of storytelling in the social life of the village, highlights the emptiness that followed the decline of the tradition of storytelling in Irish cultural society and it points to Kennelly's identification of the dual role of story in both

demolishing and sustaining a variety of urban and rural my-
thologies. The story itself is presented as the cherished prop-
erty of the storyteller, Robbie Cox, who inherited the story
like a precious family heirloom "further back than anyone
could remember" (*TBAH*, 26). The story remains significantly
anonymous in the poem, suggestive of the generic importance
of story rather than the highlighting of a specified narrative.
The organic entity that is the story grows and spreads over
twelve days and finishes on New Year's Day:

> When it was done
> The New Year was in,
> Made authentic by the story,
> The old year was dead,
> Buried by the story.
> The man endured,
> Deepened by the story. (*TBAH*, 26)

Kennelly's repetition of the phrase "by the story" empha-
sises the enabling ability of the storytellers, through their nar-
ratives, to not only fill the lives of the people with a sense of
joy and wonder but to provide a historicity in which an in-
creasingly fragmented sense of contemporary identity can find
a secure foundation. The story acts as a unifying cultural entity
that operates as a social and chronological adhesive, literally
and metaphorically bringing people together and establishing
an often ambivalent morality that in many ways defied defini-
tion outside the confines of the narrative. In her study of the
infamous burning of Brigid Cleary in Ballyvadlea, County Tip-
perary, in 1895, Angela Bourke notes the centrality of story-
telling in the construction of codes of rural behaviour and
collective identities and she alludes to the practical conse-
quences that can ensue from the literal interpretation of what
are essentially metaphoric constructions:

> Stories gain verisimilitude, and stories keep their lis-
> teners' attention by the density of circumstance they
> depict, including social relations and the details of
> work. Most stories, however, are constructed around
> the unexpected, and therefore memorable, happen-
> ings in people's lives. (Bourke, 1999: 37)

Much of Kennelly's skill as a poet derives from this story-
telling tradition in which the ability to hold the attention of an
audience is based on the degree to which the story/song/
poem attempts to reflect the experience of life as felt by the
listeners. Again, it is precisely within this tradition that Ken-
nelly's noted liking for the epic form finds its genesis and one
of the key features of his long poems, despite their disrupted
chronologies and ambivalent relationships, is the narrative
energy driving the poems forward. Kennelly clearly realises
the centrality of story in the construction of the past and its
ability to hold together often conflicting ideologies and rival
perceptions of the contemporary. Equally, he utilises the myr-
iad subversive qualities of story in the more complex and dis-
tended epics of *Cromwell, The Book of Judas* and *Poetry My Arse,*
as well as revelling in the more conventionally narrative and
picaresque poems of the Moloney sequence. Clearly, the im-
portance of stories and their crucial role in the establishment
of personal and national mythologies are central hermeneuti-
cal weapons in the Kennellian arsenal.

Kennelly grew up in a village and a pub that cherished its
music and its storytellers and had a strong sense of commu-
nity, even if this did occasionally spill over into faction fights
associated with the passion for village Gaelic Football. Poetry,
according to Kennelly, in many ways fills the gap between
storytelling and singing with its combination of rhythm, pitch,
tone and subject. He remembers the respect shown to the
singers in his father's pub where a magical silence would de-
scend on the usually noisy pub when a singer rose. In many

ways, singing crossed every social barrier that existed be-
tween people, with pride of place being reserved for those
who had mastered a particular song and almost made it their
own. "Living Ghosts" presents the songs heard by Kennelly in
the pub, and elsewhere, as entities reincarnated in the hearts
and mouth of the singers and acquiring transcendental prop-
erties through their expression. The songs exist as haun-
tological connections between generations, manufacturing
bridges that link communities and individuals across the re-
strictions of linear time :

> I've seen men in their innocence
> Untroubled by right and wrong.
> I close my eyes and see them
> Becoming song.
>
> All the songs are living ghosts
> And long for a living voice.
> O may another fall of snow
> Bid Broderick rejoice. (*TBAH*, 38)

These songs are celebrations, laments and reveries that
completely transform the singers and allow them to escape
into a world in which the unwritten rules that govern their
lives can be ignored, and there are strong parallels between
Kennelly's depiction of the social role and standing of the
singer and the storyteller. The effect of these songs on those
who heard them is captured in "The Singing Girl is Easy in
her Skill", a poem first published in 1979, but included in *The
Boats Are Home* because of its depiction of the restorative
cultural properties of song. When listening to a girl who is a
confident and beautiful singer, Kennelly notes "we are more
human then we were before" (*TBAH*, 41). The song has in-
duced a calm over those who are listening and in that precise
moment "we cannot see just now why men should kill". The
singing has anaesthetised the listeners and through its pure

beauty and perfection of form has induced the feeling that people too can somehow reflect this perfection in the way they treat others. The possibility of perfection, and indeed redemption, is raised by the form of the song and that is its ultimate value. In many ways, however, the singing is a futile exercise because it cannot actually change anything and those listening are aware of this. What it offers is hope, and that is more than enough, in Kennelly's mind, to justify its existence.

Perhaps the dominant image of *The Boats Are Home* is that of a violence that permeates all aspects of existence and consequently each stratum of society. This violence manifests itself in an obvious physical aggression and in the subtle, more sinister guise of those people entrusted with authority or influence. In his essay "Poetry and Violence", Kennelly muses over his translation of Eileen O'Connell's eighteenth-century ballad *A Cry for Art O'Leary*, a poem he admires for its "violence — sexual, religious, political, forms of violence that occur again and again throughout Irish writing" (Kennelly, 1994: 23). Kennelly certainly does not shirk from portraying the various manifestations of violence in his society and *The Boats Are Home* points to a subtler but no less dangerous psychological and emotional violence inflicted on children by the very people chosen by society to protect and cherish its young. The impression created by the collection is of an entire generation growing up despite of and not thanks to the very institutions created to enable their transition into adulthood and it is this pervading sense of the betrayal of trust on such a huge scale that led Kennelly to overtly explore the notion of betrayal a decade later in *The Book of Judas*. The dominant forces of church and state allowed little or no tolerance for deviance from a strictly imposed moral code, one that was shown to be laced with hypocrisy by revelations of widespread clerical child sex abuse in the 1990s. Indeed, Kennelly's poetry certainly hints at the scandal of child abuse

long before such revelations became relatively commonplace.
He recalls the chief characteristics of this time as:

> The repression in the church, the suicides of girls, the
> schools, the brutal teachers, the notion that a boy
> could get fifty slaps on the hand for stammering or for
> writing with his left hand, the total lack of any sexual
> education – these are all in retrospect comic in a way,
> but at the time you're going through it, it was very
> puzzling. (Pine, 1990: 21)

The Boats are Home presents the primary school not as a
place of engagement and learning, but of fear, repression and
brutality. In the opening poem, entitled "To Learn", Kennelly
contrasts the impression made on a young boy by the nine
fields that lay between his house and the school. Each field is
filled by the boy's imagination which is triggered by the differ-
ent quality of land in each or by an animal which occupies it.
The poem celebrates the wonder of a young boy who recre-
ates his expanding world with images of familiarity and whose
imagination can inspire both happiness and fear by the mere
act of peering through a hedge. The "real" process of learning
has been active throughout the journey to school but it is a
process that is not recognised by the regime of the class-
room. The inorganic school stands out against the lushness of
the colour of the fields in which it is set, and "the gravelly
rise" on which the school is built presents education as a
hard and stony process that reflects the physical difficulty of
getting to the school. Kennelly concludes the poem thus:

> He thought of the nine fields in turn
> As he beat the last ditch and came
> In sight of the school on the gravelly rise.
> He buckled down to learn. (*TBAH*, 9)

The last line neatly draws the boundary between the mys-
terious world of the nine fields, created in the freedom of the

boy's imagination, and the stifling nature of the world pre-
sented by people with no other desire than to control a
roomful of children. Kennelly is not attempting to create a
stereotypical view of education in which all teachers are cruel
and insensitive but he is reflecting a view of education that can
be regularly found in Irish literature from the anecdotal *An-
gela's Ashes* by Frank McCourt to the sheer violence and bru-
tality of *Nothing to Say* by Mannix Flynn. The final line,
"buckling down to learn", is carefully chosen to highlight the
weight placed on young children by a violent and insensitive
educational system. The dual meaning of the word "buckle" is
intended to portray the leather belt that was the most memo-
rable educational symbol for thousands of young children as
well as the buckling of the individual under the repression of
the pedagogical regime. Many of those who entered teaching
did not do so out of a genuine vocation or desire to teach but
rather because they were seeking the economic security and
social respectability of a teaching position. Kennelly describes
his first teacher in far from flattering terms:

> "Instead of finding security, all they found was mental
> frustration and bewilderment. The teacher didn't
> want to know, didn't want to feel the uncertainties of
> the students at all and all I remember out of that class
> was fear, beatings, crying, sticks and shouting — vio-
> lence. I think I derive a lot of my thought from him,
> the opposite." (Murphy, 1987: 49)

The effect of such an education is reflected in the cold, dis-
passionate and somewhat detached tone of much of the poetry
he has written concerning this part of his life. There is not
much hope in the poetic depiction of the educational experi-
ences of these children in *The Boats Are Home*, nor are there
many of Kennelly's humorous insights, typified by the Moloney
sequence, that enliven his depiction of the people of Ballylong-
ford and its environs. The effect of the teacher's "betrayal" of

his role seems to be Kennelly's quiet but determined effort to record the tragedy of the classroom in concrete language and images that unambiguously articulate their own clear meaning. "The Stick" is an excellent example of Kennelly's practised skill in distilling the essence of a moment through the careful recalling of events in such a way as to imbue the simple form with an air of menace and threat, exemplified by the again anonymous "man", an austere and menacing presence:

> And with the knife sculpted
> A thin hard stick, his work of art.
> Back in the room, he looked at the boy's faces.
> They'd be farmers, labourers, even singers, fiddlers, dancers.
> He placed the stick on the mantelpiece above the fire.
> His days were listening to boys' voices
> Who'd know the stick if they didn't know the answers.
>   (*TBAH*, 12)

The real damage that Kennelly highlights is the association of the lack of knowledge with physical punishment. Pupils who did not provide the answer would spend their days in abject fear of being asked a question and most of what they did learn was for the sake of the avoidance of a beating rather than through any inquisitorial drive.

The association of the place of learning with violence appears so natural to the children that violence itself is legitimised through the behaviour of the teacher while the children's internalisation of this violence is realised in their later behaviour. This violence enters all aspects of their relationships with people, their surroundings and the animals who share that environment and it creates an inner aggression that appears to gnaw away at the heart of those exposed to it. The pointlessness of this educational violence is hinted at by Kennelly when he notes that "they'd be farmers, labourers, even singers, fiddlers, dancers", indicating that despite the fear engendered by the teacher, the boys would live their lives according to the economic circumstances that would prevail, and they would enjoy the delights of singing, music and dancing while another generation of children, probably their own, suffered the humiliation and degradation that passed for education. Kennelly does not depict the teacher as a victim of the same educational system which is inflicted on the children but more as an instigator of violence with "a thin hard stick, his work of art". He allows no sympathy for the teacher, indicating the long-lasting effect of the mental and physical violence on the children.

"The Stick" is an excellent example of the complex nature of Kennelly's poetic style, combining free verse and the fourteen-line sonnet, so effectively utilised throughout his work, to produce a poem that is both compact and free-flowing. Equally, the influence of the oral tradition on Kennelly's poetry can be clearly seen in his careful balancing of phrases and lines that reflect the natural cadence of local speech. He also carefully measures the relative lengths and importance of individual lines to attune the poem to its most important recipient, the ear of the listener. The subtle use of rhymes ("dancers" / "answers") act as a musical undercurrent to the poem while also indicating the ironic relationship between the two words. The manufacturing of the icon of repression, the stick, involves a gradual accretion of tension upon the alliterated repetition of the initial sound of the stick ("stirred", "strip", "size", "shape", "sculpted", "stick") and the overall effect of this deliberated attention to form is to allow the poem to conform as much as possible to Kennelly's fervently held belief in the centrality of the listener.

The complexities of Kennelly's response to the harsh treatment he received at the hands of some of his teachers gives rise to the bitterness and anger of poems such as "A Return" and to the sadness of "The Brightest of All". "A Return" is similar in its treatment of the dominating influences in an individual's life to "Measures", the opening statement in

Cromwell, in that both poems open the present mind of the poetic voice to those who have shaped its development, either indirectly, as in the case of Oliver Cromwell, or directly, as in the face of the teacher who occupies Kennelly's dream. "A Return" is one of Kennelly's angriest poems in that not only does he resent the appearance of a hated teacher who had been "convinced that every child is a brat of parasite" (*BS,* 16) but, unlike the dialogic exchanges of *Cromwell, The Book of Judas* and *The Man Made of Rain,* there is no bartering, no tentative sharing of memories or careful mapping of possible routes of resolution. The poem is particularly noteworthy in the prominence given to a dream and to the poet's difficult and confrontational relationship with it as this is a central and recurring technique in Kennelly's poetry. His response reflects the depth of emotion touched by the memory of this man:

> I feel again a wave of hate
> Begin to drown my mind and there
> In the struggle arena, I rise, I live,
> Amazed at the obscenities scalding my lips,
> Untouched when his great head cowers
> Then lifts — O God, that unforgettable shape —
> Begging the pardon that I will not give. (*BS,* 16)

What Kennelly is exploring in this poem is quite different from the clinical violence of "The Stick". At the time of their reception, the beatings and humiliations appeared as a natural part of schooling to the boys. However, the realisation, later in life, that violence was not necessarily an integral part of the learning process undoubtedly leads to a questioning of the effects of this violence on the individual. In his dreams Kennelly is exacting his revenge over the teacher by refusing the forgiveness that is being sought but he is concurrently angry that the figure of the teacher can so easily stride into his subconscious and once again dominate his mind. However, because this forgiveness is being sought in the poet's subconscious mind, it can certainly be interpreted that the key to moving beyond cataclysmic events of the past is to engage in an internal act of forgiveness, however difficult that is to achieve. This idea is cemented in Buffun's desire in *Cromwell* to sit outside a pub "sipping infinite pints of cool beer" (*C*, 117) with Oliver Cromwell, a sense of resolution clearly absent from "A Return". The poem ends with the strong impression of the damage brought about by this teacher, in that the poet is not happy with the "scalding" effects of his anger and is unable to purge this anger through an imaginary forgiveness. The violence has created a world of resentment and bitterness that neither the poet nor the teacher can escape, leaving open questions rather than final answers.

Given the influence of the Catholic clergy in the shaping of the ethos of primary school education in Ireland, religious education, otherwise known as "catechism", was therefore regarded as one of the most important subjects in the entire school curriculum. Brendan Behan recounts his experiences of the preparation for the sacrament of Confirmation at the beginning of his famous short story, "The Confirmation Suit", and his experience of the preparation of this rite of passage was certainly not unusual:

> For weeks it was nothing but simony and sacrilege, and the sins crying to heaven for vengeance, the big green Catechism in our hands, walking home along the brewery wall, with a butt too, to help our wits, what is pure spirit, and don't kill that, Billser has to get a drag out of it yet, what do I mean by apostate, and hell and heaven and despair and presumption and hope. (Martin, 1987: 244)

Despite Behan's humour, this passage unveils a more sinister power struggle operating over the role of the clergy and Catholicism in the Irish education system and it is a seminal conflict explored by Kennelly in *The Boats are Home*. In *A Time for Voices*, "The Stick" is placed on the facing page of the poem "Catechism", a poem that points to the reduction of mystery and wonder to pedantic questions and answers. Coupled with the inevitable beatings it occasioned, it is little wonder that the theory of God would be associated with all the fear and hatred that went with other school subjects:

> Religion class. Mulcahy taught us God
> While he heated his arse to a winter fire
> Testing with his fingers the supple sally rod.
> "Explain the Immaculate Conception, Maguire,
> And tell us then about the Mystical Blood."
> Maguire failed. Mulcahy covered the boy's head
> With his satchel, shoved him stumbling among
> The desks, lashed his bare legs until they bled.
>
> Who goes to hell, Dineen? Kane, what's a saint?
> Doolin, what constitutes a mortal sin?
> Flynn, what of man who calls his brother a fool?
> Years killed raving questions. Kane stomped Dublin
> In policeman's boots. Flynn was afraid of himself.
> Maguire did well out of whores in Liverpool. (*ATFV*, 21)

Kennelly's recollection of the treatment handed out to Maguire is an interesting reworking of the treatment meted out to Jesus on the Via Dolorosa, "lashed" as he stumbled along with a cross on his back and the crown of thorns, rather than a satchel, on his head. This is a poem that treads the fine line between tragedy and comedy that typifies Kennelly's recollection of his youth and the balance between the past and the future is cleverly handled in this tightly constructed work. The choice of the name Maguire for one of the central characters is perhaps an echo of the protagonist of Patrick Kavanagh's *The Great Hunger* whose existence equally straddles both tragedy and comedy. As a result of his failure to explain the "mystical Blood", Maguire must shed his own blood in the inevitable beating. This intended irony highlights the gulf between what is being taught and how it is being taught and the variegated responses such treatment elicits. Kane allowed the questioning and punishment to materialise in his choice of career as a policeman, a tacit internalisation with the way in which religion was presented and an appreciation of the powerful social position of the church. Flynn, so terrified and overwhelmed by the whole violent educational experienced, is reduced to an emotional shell, suffering a form of pedagogically induced post-traumatic stress disorder. Maguire, the most obvious victim, also internalises the violence and to an extent replicates the model of morality presented to him in the classroom by profiting from the exploitation of prostitutes, cleverly juxtaposing Kane in a responsive binary. Each "raving" question, from the frightening concept of the mystical blood to the exploration of hell, sin and salvation, was answerable with a preset formula, and the consequent effects on Kennelly clearly point to the origins of his epistemological stylistics:

> "There was no discussion, only questions and answers. If a question is framed in such a way that it says to you 'I'm going to ask you about this most amazing mystery and here is the answer; you must learn off this answer and give it back to me', it's a formula for total intellectual slavery and I think it took me many years to shake off that need to give an answer." (Murphy, 1987: 52)

The nature of Kennelly's response to the negative aspects of his education appears to be a deeper understanding of the parasitical nature of oppositional forces, such as good and evil, despair and hope, right and wrong. Kennelly's personal perception of the classroom world is teased out by its negativity and violence, which then acts as a catalyst to the sensitivity already present within him. It is only through this attempted understanding of the nature of contrary beliefs that he can arrive at an attempted appraisal of the nature of these uncertain, indefinite and paradoxical beliefs. Interestingly, in his essay on the poetry of Joseph Mary Plunkett, Kennelly notes that Plunkett's poem "Heaven and Hell" is a "dream-battle" in which the dominant impulse is to "see, plainly and precisely, what exactly is evil and what is good" (Kennelly, 1994: 105) and this impulse is also clearly visible in *The Boats Are Home.*

In the poem "The Smell" Kennelly presents a more benign and organic perspective on the areas of religious faith, ritual and belief, portraying faith as something to be encountered on the level of personal contact with an open-ended experiential philosophy concerning the nature of life. Kneeling beside an old woman in a church, the six-year-old child is entranced by the mesmeric effect of the woman's whispering prayers and the lines of age on her face. The kneeling woman is dressed in black because of a personal bereavement, and is on her knees before the image of Christ on the cross:

> The rent, dumb Christ, listener at the doors of the heart
> The pummelled Christ, the sea of human pain,
> The salted Christ, the drinker of horrors,
> The prisoner Christ, dungeoned on flesh and bone.
>   (*TBAH*, 14)

It is the smell of the woman that initially transfigures the boy and allows him to transcend the inside of the church and the "pallid Christ on the cross", facilitating the realisation that the silence of the church and the figure of Christ, a dumb, battered and damaged icon, provides hope and a sense of security and identity precisely as a result of its humanity, vulnerability and weakness. The woman finally takes the young boy's hand and they leave the church together, a peculiar union of the old and the young, the bereaved and the bewildered, and a typical Kennellian symbol of a patched, odd, yet quietly determined humanity. They leave the church and enter the now purged "rain-cleaned air", the woman's mere presence having spoken to the boy "beyond lips' whispers and heart's prayers", freeing him into one of his first, tentative, confusing yet exhilarating experiences of self-revelation.

The most powerful of all the emotions expressed in Kennelly's poems concerning childhood is fear, "the fear of the unknown in people's lives, like the fear of sleep, the fear of dreams, the fear of sex, the fear of a woman or any kind of sexual love, which is very strong still in Ireland" (Murphy, 1987: 52). In the poem "Lost" Kennelly delves into an unknown fear, anger and shame that forces a child to hide from the world. The reason for the desire to "crawl away" (*TBAH*, 16) and find some place that would offer anonymity is not proffered by Kennelly but is described as "shame or hurt or whatever it was". What is important is not what the child has done but the failure of the adults to realise or respect the child's need to be alone. The house in which the child hides is described as an oxymoronic "sanctuary of dark and cold" which is breached only by the voices calling out the child's name to "come out come back come home". The need for an ever-receding solitude is a powerful theme in many of Kennelly's poems and is captured towards the end of the poem:

> And you wonder why
> Being lost in yourself should stir
> This cry in others
> Who seem together
> Behind the shadowed edges of their lives
> Their own cries slashing the air
> As the day dawns, as the day dies. (*TBAH*, 17)

This notion of people's inability to leave other people alone, many of whom desire the very solitude being denied to them, is part of Kennelly's analysis of the frustrations of childhood. "Lost" evokes the image of the individual swamped by the collective identity of the "shadowed" community and refused the right to be an individual. On the other hand, there is the security and friendship that only a community can offer and herein lies the essential ambiguity of growing up in a village where deviance from the norm is viewed with great suspicion. Part of the child's wondering is the fact that so many people are concerned about his/her welfare and the poem is full of images of pain and suffering, from "a house emptier than yourself, a raw place bleeding with memories" to the cries of the searchers "slashing the air". What is behind all these images is Kennelly's simple, yet practically impossible, desire for solitude. In "The Smell", Kennelly notes that "I opened my eyes to the silence" (*TBAH*, 14), thereby cleverly juxtaposing two sensory drives, thereby creating a paradigm of unfulfillable desire.

Alongside these more symbolic poems of isolation and loneliness, *The Boats Are Home* deals with a cruder, direct physical violence that helped establish the social pecking order in rural communities. One of the most brutal of these poems is called, quite simply, "Beatings", and in it Kennelly characteristically observes the ordinary nature of violence through a factual recording of events:

> Hannify lifted the ash butt and struck
> Quilter on the head and back.
> For a while Quilter took it standing up
> But a blow on the neck
> Grounded him. Turning over on
> His face, his hands clasped the back of his head.
> Hannify's anger seemed more than human.
> He hit Quilter till he was half-dead.
> Quilter got over it though. For six weeks
> He slunk like a hurt cur through dark and light,
> Licking his wounds till the strength returned.
> On May eve Hannify's sheepdog died.
> Five cows were poisoned at a stroke.
> No sign of Quilter when Hannify's hayshed burned.
>   (*TBAH*, 36)

The brutality of Hannify's attack is captured by Kennelly's careful attention to the length of the first eight lines so that each stage of the violence is slowed and frozen by its existence on a separate line. This also serves to highlight the deliberate and cold-blooded nature of the beating by the gradual reduction of Quilter to the foetal position of self-protection. Once again, as in "Lost", Kennelly depicts the action after the initial cause for this particular beating has been acted out and in many ways this heightens the chilling and ubiquitous nature of violence as the reader is forced to conjecture about the nature of the original provocation. Quilter has the gritty, almost cunning, instinct of survival that manifests itself firstly in his attempts to cover his head rather than risk a more serious injury by facing up to the incensed Hannify, and secondly in his willingness to wait for his revenge. This revenge is as slow and deliberate as the beating he received, but its consequences are far more severe. Quilter is shrewd enough to target three vital elements of a farmer's livelihood, increasing the satisfaction he gets from his revenge by leaving the hayshed till last. Kennelly parallels human violence with the treatment of animals in describing Quilter's beating as "more than human", while his curled-up form of self-protection mirrors his slinking "like a hurt cur". Quilter takes his initial revenge on one of Hannify's animals, thus highlighting the economic hierarchy so crucial to social demographics in rural villages. Hannify, though he undoubtedly will suspect Quilter for these attacks, will be unable to prove the association.

The question raised by this poem centres around the effects of violence, not only on the victim but also upon those who inflict the violence. In many ways this poem thematically parallels "A Return" in which Kennelly attempted but failed to forgive the violence perpetrated on him by a ruthless teacher. The desire for revenge, or at least an unwillingness to forgive, would appear to be what Kennelly has distilled as one of the major after-effects of violence. Violence kills the sensibility that would allow forgiveness and so changes the victim in a profound and dangerous way. Violence, therefore, can take many forms in the subconscious of the victim, from a belief that the beating was deserved to a carefully considered and executed revenge, as in Quilter's case, in which retribution is exacted not only for the physical but also the mental suffering and in which the original perpetrator of the violence suffers more in the long term. Because of the open-ended nature of much of his poetry Kennelly offers no solution to this violence other than an honest appraisal of the existence of revenge, fear, hatred and mistrust in the heart of every individual and the hint that through the recognition of their existence perhaps some means of coping can be found. Violence exists in Kennelly's poetry as a powerful, destructive yet intrinsically natural element in the complexity of the human psyche.

Among the dominant images in *The Boats Are Home* is the use of light and darkness as a metaphor for the experience of moving towards a fuller understanding of self. One of Kennelly's best-known early poems, "My Dark Fathers", concerns Kennelly's attempt not only to define his relationship with Irish history but somehow to locate some nodal point of darkness that is the genesis of existence and from which the individual must seek the "undeceiving" (*MDF*, 8) light. This image of light and darkness has perhaps been overloaded, through history, with religious overtones, but Kennelly's choice of light as the source of wonder and hope, and its oppositional relationship with darkness, probably relates back to his school days in which the images presented to him of what was good and what was evil usually involved a dramatic and powerful association of light with good and darkness with evil. Kennelly describes the effect of his religious education as follows:

> "It got me at the totally imagistic level of actually see-
> ing things. I think that this is really amazing — that
> your whole moral being could be expressed in those
> terms, that everything you could feel or aspire to or
> know can be expressed in these extraordinary images
> of devils and angels, saints, Heaven, Hell, Purgatory
> and Limbo. They're wonderful words, of course, and I
> think that being filled with them when you're so
> young, they never leave you. You tend to divide the
> world into heroes and villains afterwards." (Murphy,
> 1987: 21)

This tendency to "divide the world into heroes and villains" has largely been resisted by Kennelly who is very much aware of the dangers of such an easy system of definition. However, there are still traces of this childhood legacy in his poetry. In "Lost", for example, the child finds a "sanctuary of dark" in which the freedom to be alone is cherished, but is spoilt by the need for the light to seek out the child and expose its whereabouts. Darkness is the cover which not only protects those who wish to remain anonymous, but conversely har-bours danger and threat and is the source of much childhood fear. Light, on the other hand, has its own dualistic qualities in that it not only provides warmth, hope and security, but it also can result in an obtrusive desire to expose in which no-one is left alone.

In "The Brightest of All" Kennelly recalls his attempt to assimilate the story of Lucifer's "piteous, fabulous" fall from grace, which was told in terms of a fall from the brightness of the sun into the darkness of the centre of the earth. The im-age created in Kennelly's mind is of a tremendous brightness trapped in the "secret heart" (*TBAH*, 11) of the earth, and as a boy he hoped that one ray of light from this heart would come and lessen the pain in the varicose legs of Sean McCarthy, the teacher who recounted the story. This secret heart, full of a healing brightness, is not a "deep prison" that is hidden from the world and it is interesting given Kennelly's liking of those who occupy the margins of history that the fallen angel is the brightest. The paradox in the poem is that the fallen angel is depicted as the brightest of all while God is presented as an angry entity, thus transposing the usual format of good and evil in an attempt to explore the nature of evil as it is presented through the image of Lucifer.

In "Dream of a Black Fox" the black fox is depicted as the "lord of darkness" (*DBF*, 51) that rules his sleep. Yet, in this poem, Kennelly points to the illusory nature of these nocturnal creations as that which "makes fear a part of pure creation", hinting that it is in the "light" that the individual will come closest to peace. This also suggests that the association between night and evil, darkness and terror, is based on groundless fears created in the imagination. His skill as a poet is to create images of intense darkness, a black world of dangerous dreams and fearful thoughts, and to emerge from these "into the light" and the hope that is born out of the former experience.

Perhaps the key to these images lies in the connection made between this metaphorical darkness and light, and this is the theme explored by Kennelly in the poem "Connection", published in *The Voices* in 1973, in which the search for meaning is contained in those few brief moments of illumination:

> Connect the desert with the sun at noon
> Revealing open beaks, descending wings
> And bones that hint of spirits that are free.
> We open in a moment, love, and then
> Linked with the livingness of growing things
> Express the shell and comprehend the sea. (*TV*, 9)

In the introduction to *A Time for Voices*, Kennelly describes the poem "Yes", first published in *The Boats Are Home*, as a poem "born of positive feeling connected with the brutality of the other poems" (*ATFV*, 12). The connection is made, in the poem, between the "agony" (*TBAH*, 37) that often precedes the ability to be positive and the determination that results in this affirmative utterance. The brutality witnessed by Kennelly in the course of his primary education has elicited a variety of responses but the most difficult reaction to make is one that sees a positive aspect in all this negativity, but in "Yes" this aspect is born directly out of the struggle with the violence and the poet's determination not to allow this aggression to become an intrinsic part of his nature. In "A Return", Kennelly provided an insight into the difficulty involved in the assimilation of his past when the image of his brutal teacher returns seeking forgiveness that Kennelly is unable to provide. His abject inability to say yes to the image hints at the agony and trauma that lies behind this simple, affirmative word. Kennelly is not suggesting that oppositional notions, and words such as yes and no, are fixed positions into which an individual naturally slips but are concepts that cannot be regarded as definitive absolutes. "Yes" and "No" are fluid perspectives that the individual struggles to interpret and he argues in the poem that even though, on occasions, it is impossible to say yes, a reinterpretation of what he terms "agony" can provide a more positive and constructive outlook on life.

"Yes" is an ageless word, the last word of Molly Bloom's soliloquy that concludes James Joyce's *Ulysses*, and a declaration of Kennelly's often-expressed desire for perpetual reinvention of the self. Despite the dark nature of a good deal of Kennelly's work, there is a constant undercurrent of belligerent positivity that asserts an almost Darwinian belief in the ability of the human spirit to triumph over adversity. In an insightful essay on Joyce, Kennelly celebrates Joyce's "humanism" which he characterises as "candour" (Kennelly, 1994: 224), a delicate artistic balance between subjective honesty and literary style. Indeed, in his depiction of Leopold Bloom,

Kennelly refers to the fact that "he is made vulnerable, discriminating and reflective through being endlessly impinged upon, entered into" (Kennelly, 1994: 228), a portrayal that could equally apply to Buffun, the troubled protagonist of *Cromwell*. "Yes" clearly points to Kennelly's conscious and studied belief in Joyce's constant struggle against "the desperation fostered by familiarity" (Kennelly, 1994: 225):

> I am always beginning to appreciate
> The agony from which it is born.
> Clues from here and there
> Suggest such agony is hard to bear
> But is the shaping God
> Of the word that we
> Sometimes hear, and struggle to be. (*TBAH*, 37)

The Boats Are Home explores many aspects of rural Irish life, from the affirming talents of singers and storytellers, to rituals surrounding everyday life, to the equally important rituals associated with death in Ireland, such as the traditional visits by relatives and friends to the house of the deceased, and the wake, in which family and friends get together to celebrate the life of the dead person, essentially articulating a positive approach to the inevitability of death. "The Gift Returned" provides an insight into Kennelly's approach to the subject of death and it is a thoughtful, carefully constructed poem concerning the reflections of a son as he bears his mother's coffin, with the help of his brothers, towards her grave. The description of the corpse's "deadweight" as "the lightest thing imaginable" echoes Kennelly's description of the origin of his poetic ability as "small and hesitant" in "The Gift", the two images united by a sense of the sublime nature of our most important emotional responses. Both poems present the fragile nature of self-perception, shaped as it is by people and forces largely beyond our immediate control, their significance barely achieving articulation. There is also the image of the gift, earlier described as a hesitant small child, now being returned to the ground in the shape of the child's mother, a statement of concurrent independence and gratitude, a recognition of where the voice has come from and a declaration that from now on the voice is on its own.

Kennelly's strength once again lies in his ability to pinpoint a specific chronological moment in which a potentially amorphous memory is preserved, and this is described early in the poem with the recollection of the narrator's brother's breathing as they carried the coffin. This breathing haunts the poem as a dual symbol of the existence of life and a memory of the traumatic effect of death on a person close to the deceased. There is a strong connection in the poem between the dead body and the earth in which it will finally rest in which Kennelly emphasises the organic connection between human existence and nature. The "return" he describes is one of a reciprocal nature, in which the dead person shows their gratitude for life through a unification of their "skulls and bones" with the "patient grass" and the "sense of leaving" that is such a strong part of the experience of death is alleviated by this "sense of returning". The language of the poem is dominated by religious symbolism and metaphors, principal amongst which is the belief in a life after death and the notion of a "promised land" that is composed of "love". Kennelly appears to move comfortably in these images, imbuing them with his personal reflections and the gritty determination of those he grew up with to face life in as positive a fashion as possible, and this inevitably includes a belief in death as part of the cycle of life and as such it loses whatever fear it might have. Kennelly's sense of God is exactly that of his sense of the poetic function, namely a belief in "the hope of connection both with oneself and with the outside world" (Kennelly, 1990: 12) and the poem can be regarded as a clear testament to survival and the regenerative spirit. He concludes the poem as follows:

> Yet it was there in the patient grass.
> In her final silence,
> In his brothers' breathing,
> In the place authentic beyond words
> Where the sense of returning
> Swallowed the sense of leaving. (*TBAH*, 23)

The poem is written in the third person and highlights the ease with which Kennelly shifts the narrative emphasis throughout the collection from the first person to the third person to the objective narrator. This creates the intended dislocation of authorial identification with the articulated voice, and this is compounded by Kennelly's assertion that "by saying 'I' in such poems I experience a genuine sense of freedom, of liberating myself from my self" (*ATFV*, 12). This shifting perspective in the collection allows Kennelly to both personalise and universalise without directly limiting his freedom by too close an identification with any particular viewpoint and this poetic anonymity is an essential element in his poetic vision as it allows many "voices" to roam freely within the boundaries of his expression. In some ways Kennelly is closely adhering to Roland's Barthes's assumption that "the birth of the reader must be at the cost of the death of the author" (Lodge, 1988: 172) in that he wishes his poetry to be, in theory and in practice, a "flight from this deadening authoritative egotism" that seeks to "seduce/ambush us all into upright, respectable, 'mature', competent corpses giving instructions to our youthful better" (*ATFV*, 12). This freedom is achieved through Kennelly's willingness and ability to shift the narrative of his poems and to vary the subject matter that each poem addresses.

The final poem in *The Boats Are Home* acts as a résumé of childhood and educational experiences and their consequent effects in later life. In six sonnets under the collective title "Six of One", Kennelly describes the characteristics of a variety of recognisable manifestations of self. The title, however, raises the question as to whether these six characters exist independently in individual people or whether they are, in fact, elements of the individual psyche that operate at varying levels. The six cameos describe the qualities of, amongst others, the self-styled "expert" and the self-satisfied "barbarian". "The Expert" is a biting satirical poem in which Kennelly attacks the attitude of those who seek to circumscribe what passes for education:

> The area is limited, it is true.
> His knowledge of the area is not.
> Right from the start, he knows what to do
> And how to do it. All the fish he caught
> Were salmon of knowledge and not once
> Did he burn his thumb although he touched the fire
> Of minds zealous as his own. God's a dunce
> When the expert pronounces in his sphere
> For he has scoured the fecund libraries
> Till each one yielded all its special riches.
> Prometheus, overworked and undersexed,
> Files in his mind the succulent clarities
> Knowing, from the ways of pricks and bitches,
> Living is a footnote to the authentic text. (*TBAH*, 52)

This powerful image of the expert as Prometheus stealing the fire of true knowledge from the fertile libraries and replacing it with his prosaic and bloated deliberations hints at a certain anti-intellectualism in Kennelly's poetry. However, what he is pointing to in the poem is the danger of perceiving secondary opinions and ideas without the essential correlative of an intellectual generosity that would acknowledge other perspectives and it is precisely this type of generosity that characterises Kennelly's work through the constant articulation of voices other than his own. The "expert", far from attempting to add to the store of human knowledge, exists in a world devoted to self-promotion and is fatally wounded by the refusal to acknowledge that this sea of knowledge is, in fact, to use Kennelly's terminology, teeming with other fish besides himself. The last line of the poem points to Kennelly's belief that literature is born out of the desire to express the extraordinary complexity and magnificence of existence. "The Expert" typifies many of the faults in the educational system, including the narrowness of the curriculum and the lack of personal sensitivity towards pupils, that Kennelly has portrayed throughout *The Boats Are Home*.

The other characters in "Six of One", from the misguided warrior "pregnant with honour in service to The Cause" to the arrogant missionary declaring "And on behalf of God I say, that's right", are those people unable to see beyond the self-imposed limits of their understanding and who regard those who disagree with them with a mixture of pity and derision. Kennelly's early education, as portrayed in these collections, has resulted in the strong image of and fascination with the narrow-mindedness that exemplifies "Six of One". These characters are deliberately stereotyped to highlight their salient features which can be summarised as the inability to look beyond the boundaries that they themselves have set. "The Missionary" highlights the violence perpetrated on innocent people in the name of Jesus Christ, and Kennelly links the brutality and insensitivity of the missionary with the religious education he received at school. Interestingly, in his essay on *Cromwell*, the perceptive Gerald Dawe draws strong connections between "Six of One" and the portrayal of Oliver Cromwell in Kennelly's long poem of the same name. He notes:

> Here in the use of an ironic persona who bases his power to impose his will upon others on a claim to divine right, Kennelly has produced the blueprint of the character of Cromwell as he is presented, or presents himself, in Kennelly's later book. (Pine, 1994: 69)

"Proof" is a powerful and revealing insight into the poet's attitude towards education and the nature of an individual's acquisition of knowledge. Experience of the extremes that life has to offer, from the joy of the sun's scattered rays to the despair and violence of a fox's desire to survive, is the route that Kennelly espouses towards true fullness of being. The image of the bleeding earth hints at the violence and suffering that lies at the heart of many of these experiences. He denounces those, like Dickens's Mr M'Choakumchild, who would claim "This is fact. This is taste" (Dickens, 1977: 15). Self-discovery and self-definition are two states that are not easily arrived at, and it can be claimed that both goals that can never be achieved but only hinted at. Kennelly argues, however, that it is precisely in and through the search for these elusive prizes that the individual can find a serenity based on an acceptance of the primacy of the searching process:

> I would like all things to be free of me,
> Never to murder the days with presupposition,
> Never to feel they suffer the imposition
> Of having to be this or that. How easy
> It is to maim the moment
> With expectation, to force it to define
> Itself. Beyond all that I am, the sun
> Scatters its light as though by accident.
>
> The fox eats its own leg in the trap
> To go free. As it limps through the grass
> The earth itself appears to bleed.
> When the morning light comes up
> Who knows what suffering midnight was?
> Proof is what I do not need. (*ATFV*, 101)

Kennelly's descriptions of the negativity of his early education unveils the perpetual existence of oppositional forces that are at play in human interaction. His exploration of the violence, mental cruelty and lack of understanding that epitomised much of this time at school transgresses their finite limits and leads him to a fuller understanding of the nature, and indeed the emotional necessity of, positive, open-ended, pupil-centred education. In order fully to explore the nature of his own emotions Kennelly delves deeply into each experience and focuses on a single, clear and identifiable image, such as the teacher's stick or the hapless, stumbling, bleeding Maguire, and from this powerful, central image he carefully and skilfully articulates the contradictions, hypocrisies and deliberate falsifications inherent in these experiences. One of the most effective of these images comes from the "The Stick" in which each apparent paradox acts like a domino when it sets off a whole series of oppositional emotions and sensations that Kennelly is forced to deal with. The classroom, supposedly the place of learning, soon becomes the place of fear and violence where the children's innate wonder at the process of learning is dulled by the presentation of ready-made, uncritical questions and answers. The children are not beaten because they do not understand but because they have failed to rote-learn the answers. However, the collection, and Kennelly's work as a whole, does not simply present life as a series of irresolvable contradictions but rather stands as a testimony to the survival instinct of the human psyche. It is in this gritty determination to carry on regardless that the essence of a community or individual is found and no matter how negative the childhood experience, the poems exhibit an irrepressible urge to seek the positive, the good.

This hope is, however, predicated upon a sophisticated understanding of the origin of negativity, what Kennelly refers to as "poems born of *positive* feeling *connected* with the brutality of the other poems" (*ATFV*, 12). The clarity of many of the poems facilitates the reader's identification with the experience, yet this very clarity is not easily arrived at. To achieve it, Kennelly has paid very close attention to the form of the poems, with particular emphasis on line structure and length, subtle rhythms and half-rhythms. This concentration on form gives the poems a tautness and compactness that conveys the often sharp and direct nature of the poetic subject. In the best poems, Kennelly is brief, to the point and directly focused on one dominant image around which he builds his poem. Indeed, the title of the collection refers to seminal moments of self-discovery, the image of the wandering boat returning home safely with its cargo and occupants mirroring the individual's gradual and often haphazard accumulation of a concept of self. It is a clever title that unifies the sense of adventure, danger and innovation understood by the travels of the boats with the security of home, implying that the quality of the latter is dependant upon the nature of the former.

The power, cohesiveness and effectiveness of *The Boats Are Home* relies on Kennelly's use of spare language, at times sensual and soothing, at others brutal and cutting, combining the skill of the storyteller with that of the practised and shrewd observer. The process of learning is an innate one that is not reliant upon formal educational structures, against which it often reacts; the imagination, in all its freedom and boundless energy, is the real educator. Kennelly begins *The Boats Are Home* with a poem concerning the transformative abilities of the imagination, which is central to his theory of learning, and concludes it with a portrayal of the potentially devastating consequences on those to whom this freedom is denied.

Chapter Three

Spilling Selves: *Cromwell*

> I began by suggesting that my point of view involved
> poetry as divination, as a restoration of the culture to
> itself. In Ireland in this century it has involved for
> Yeats and many others an attempt to define and in-
> terpret the present by bringing it into significant rela-
> tionship with the past, and I believe that effort in our
> present circumstances has to be urgently renewed.
> (Heaney, 1980: 60)

Seamus Heaney's identification of the function of poetry in
the Irish setting has a particular significance in relation to
Kennelly's 1983 epic sequence *Cromwell*, an extraordinary
poem that seeks to bring major historical events and charac-
ters from Ireland's colonial past into direct confrontation
with the polyvocal, multivalent postcolonial present through
the imagination of the poem's protagonist, M.P.G.M. Buffun.
First published by Beaver Row Press in 1983, then reprinted
by Bloodaxe Books in 1987, the poem explores the voices
occupying the troubled conscious and subconscious mind of
Buffun, a man whose identity is shaped as much by the ghosts
of the past as by the symbols and icons of the present. The
poem is hugely significant in the development of not only the
hermeneutics of contemporary Irish poetry but also in the

radical and dislocatory methodologies employed by Kennelly in pursuit of his goal. The poem stands head and shoulders above any contemporary work in the breadth of its vision and the extent of its enquiry into the complex nature of Ireland's postcolonial identity and as such requires a detailed analysis.

Kennelly presents his version of "the nightmare of Irish history" (*C*, 7) through the dreams and reveries of Buffun, a human conglomeration whose imagination is populated by such disparate characters as, amongst others, his mother, Edmund Spenser, William of Orange and the dominant figure of Oliver Cromwell. It is only by engaging in an often surreal dialogue with these figures that Buffun can come to terms with the forces and characters that have helped shape his confused and battered identity, and through this dialogue Buffun becomes a mirror through which a confused, prejudiced and highly contentious image not only of his personal identity but of a larger Irish national identity begins to emerge. Kennelly's aim in the poem is not to consciously "forge the uncreated conscience of the race" but rather to explore and express the many conflicting voices that in the postcolonial Irish context struggle to express competing versions of national identity. He is also developing an interest in Oliver Cromwell which pre-dates his epic poem and there are indications in earlier poetry of the seminal influence of Cromwell on Kennelly's psyche and his overwhelming need to confront his perceptions of this influential historical figure.

In a previously unpublished and highly significant poem entitled "Oliver Cromwell Looks at an Irish Actor Playing the Part of Oliver Cromwell", Kennelly engages in precisely the kind of dialogue that typifies *Cromwell*, namely a challenging of hegemonic interpretations of complex historical events and personalities. This important long poem points to Kennelly's long-held fascination with Oliver Cromwell and Kennelly has commented that "I see now that the very title tells me I was interested in a difficult, challenging perspective" (private correspondence, I

April 1996). This illustrates the germination of his interest in the dialogic approach to history that characterises the book and the poem gives an early airing to Oliver Cromwell's theodicy, which is such a strong feature of the later epic collection. Equally, the poem indicates the religious quagmire of self-authentication that has bedevilled interpretations of Irish history, a quagmire that is regularly revisited in *Cromwell*. For example, in the poem, Oliver laments an actor's attempt to imitate him:

> In the name of the Saviour
> Who could ever imitate
> Me? Who could know the mind
> That spoke to God and did His work
> Where mad, barbaric blood
> defiled the ground that I was sent
> To cleanse and conquer? This was no dramatic
> Illusion. This was the real thing.

Cromwell voices significant historical figures and seeks not to replace the symbols and manifestations of national self-perception, but merely to propound the theory that the myths that underpin various ideologies are themselves sources of conflict and consequently open to hermeneutical disputations. Kennelly's poem brings Ireland's violent colonial past into direct confrontation and dialogue with the present "in all its bloody contradictions and bloody consistencies" (Murphy, 1987: 11). The poem does not advocate an abandonment of history but rather presents a re-reading of vital cultural touchstones in order to understand better the complex nature of contemporary models of identity. It is arguably the most significant and important twentieth-century Irish poem to attempt to move beyond what Edna Longley refers to as "the incestuous Irish anger" (Longley, 1991: 21) into a troubled, conflicting yet questioning environment where Buffún's personal journey and growth mirrors a national maturation and reawakening.

There are, of course, earlier poems in which Kennelly has explored the occupier/occupied dialectic. Poems such as "The Visitor" (*ATFV*, 41–4; originally published in *The Visitor*) and "The House That Jack Didn't Build" (*HJDB*, 10–13) present images of powerful figures whose personal surety of presence in their hosts' environment contrasts sharply with the inarticulate, confused uncertainty that their presence arouses.

In the course of his career, Kennelly has produced eight long poems, beginning with *Love Cry* in 1972 and culminating most recently with *The Man Made of Rain* in 1998 and it is a form that affords him the opportunity to explore his overarching themes in some depth. Of *The Book of Judas* Kennelly has written that he "was pushed into a far deeper scrutiny of betrayal" (*BS*, 12) which can only be achieved by adopting the form of the long poem and thus his expressed poetic drive of "entering into" characters such as Judas and Oliver Cromwell can be realised. For Kennelly, the epic form, however loosely that form is interpreted and utilised, clearly offers a poetic vehicle in which he feels that he can explore his respective characters and plots in a dynamic, thorough, critical and wide-ranging style. Given that "there is only one thing which can master the perplexed stuff of epic material into unity, and that is an ability to see in particular human experience some significant symbolism of man's general theory" (Abercrombie, 1922: 55), Kennelly utilises the epic form to tease out the nature of what he refers to as the "selfswamp" (*BS*, 11). The epic form facilitates an exfoliation of the protagonist's experiences and reflections, thus allowing the poet to elucidate the underlying themes that permeate the poem. The length of the epic form aids a depth of analysis that is essential to the examination of complex concepts such as personal and national identity. This depth is a crucial element in the overall critical effectiveness of the text and this preference for the epic form links Kennelly to an older tradition of Irish epic poetry. This tradition, according to Douglas Hyde, can be traced back to the Celtic verses of the Red Branch and Fenian cycles of the eighth and ninth centuries:

> That the Irish had already made some approach to the construction of a great epic is evident from the way in which they attempted, from a very early date, to group a number of minor sagas, which were evidently independent in their origin, round their great saga the Táin Bó Cuailnge. (Hyde, 1899: 400)

Indeed, Kennelly has acknowledged the influence of the most important modern Irish epic poem, Patrick Kavanagh's 1942 epic *The Great Hunger*, on not only his liking for the genre but also on his early poetic development. Kavanagh presents powerful images of the nature of Patrick Maguire's repressed existence while utilising an occasionally intrusive narrator that sometimes blurs the distinction between narrator and poet. Arguably, part of Kennelly's attraction to the poem lies in the constant displacement of the generic conventions, disruptions that Antoinette Quinn has described:

> Formally, *The Great Hunger* is even more versatile and varied than its fourteen-part structure might suggest, most parts consisting of a montage of different sequences, with successive sequences separated by paragraphing as well as by variations in line length, rhyming and rhythmic patterns. (Quinn, 1991: 142)

Cromwell, on the other hand, goes much further in the displacement of the formal structure of the epic with a phalanx of narrators pushing to be heard through Buffun's troubled subconscious mind. Chronology is plastic and distended, shifting both in time and space in consecutive poems, while Kennelly experiments internally with the structure of the sonnet. Buffun does not emerge from *Cromwell* as a figure of tragic pity, but rather as a multiplicity of figures, expressed in his pithy observation that "I spill my selves" (*C*, 159). Kennelly holds 254 individual poems together under the generic title of the work, juxtaposing conflicting ideologies, histories and individuals, hosting what Jonathan Allison lyrically refers to as "a democratic parliament of tongues" (Pine, 1994: 69).

In the post-structuralist era, according to Terry Eagleton,

> Literature is that realm in which the reader finds himself suspended between a "literal" and a figurative meaning, unable to choose between the two, and thus cast dizzyingly into a bottomless linguistic abyss by a text which has become "unreadable". (Eagleton, 1983: 145)

There are many instances of this linguistic, structural and chronological freefall in *Cromwell*. Kennelly develops and expands the epic form almost to the point where it deconstructs itself, yet the very lack of a fixed form reinforces Kennelly's subversive intention in *Cromwell* and enhances the overall mood of disruption and questioning that characterises the text. *Cromwell* can be seen as a central poetic contribution to a vital cultural and political reappraisal identified by Terence Brown in 1991:

> It is, I believe, imperative that, North and South, we begin to examine honestly and openly the nature of our involvement with the neighbouring island of Britain. This I consider an imperative for national health: for a society and a culture which assiduously ignores or suppresses central facts about its existence is open to enfeebling self-delusions and consequent exploitation. (Brown, 1991: 82)

Cromwell is a collection of 254 poems that are thematically linked, yet the collection does not qualify as a traditional epic in that it is divided into individual poems which utilise a variety of narrative techniques. Kennelly deliberately manipulates the epic structure in *Cromwell* by upsetting traditional forms, much as he attempts to upset traditional perceptions of history and identity in the poems. Indeed, *Cromwell* provided critics with a good deal of difficulty as to its specific nature on publication. Edna Longley refers to it, somewhat confusingly, as both "a public poem" (Longley, 1984: 21) and "an epic sequence" (Longley, 1987: 47), while Mark Patrick Hederman simply notes it as "this poem" (Hederman, 1984: 15); perhaps somewhere between these two views lies a hybrid form which reflects Kennelly's intention to dislocate the mind of the reader. Interestingly, in her review, Edna Longley notes that "Kennelly derives his aesthetics from what was liberatingly expansive in Kavanagh's *The Great Hunger*" and that "*Cromwell* also derives from the social critique which Kavanagh directed at the new Southern state, and from the culturally specific idioms in which he cast that critique" (Longley, *Poetry Review* (Date unknown), p. 47). While utilising a central narrator and following a thematic progression throughout the poems, Kennelly dislocates the narrative by articulating, at random, a variety of voices, some clearly recognisable as Buffun's and others distinctly not. Buffun does not control the voices that are articulated despite the fact that they are mainly engaged in a dialogue with his conscious and subconscious mind. This is reflective of Kennelly's view that "poetry must always be a flight from the deadening authoritative egotism and must find its voices in the byways, laneways, backyards, nooks and crannies of self" (*ATFV*, 12).

While the over-arching theme remains the perception of Oliver Cromwell in Irish history, there are few strands that hold the poems together in a recognisable epic form. The chronological progression in the poem, for example, is also disjointed, thereby forcing the reader to engage in a direct comparative exercise between the respective eras. This expansion and dislocation of the epic form complements Kennelly's unconventional approach to his subject and allows the variety of voices occupying Buffun's mind to wander at will through history and through his painful attempts at self-definition.

Of the 254 poems in *Cromwell*, 213 are written in a recognisable fourteen-line sonnet form, but again Kennelly disrupts the conventional fourteen-line iambic pentameter sonnet by upsetting the rhythm and rhyme within the lines and by deconstructing the form within the imagination of Buffun. The sonnets give the poems a loose structure within which his potentially rambling subconscious can be more easily articulated and consequently understood. However, the freedom of expression that is so vital to the poems is maintained by Kennelly's constant reworking of the poems within the fourteen-line format. It could be argued that Kennelly is attempting to reappropriate the sonnet, a classic Elizabethan poetic form, from its historical origins by reinventing it in contemporary postmodern conditions, much as he attempts to do with history itself.

Frank Kermode notes that "the Elizabethan literary debates frequently centred on the ways in which style should mirror intention" (Hollander and Kermode, 1973: 15) and Kennelly's use of sonnets would appear to mirror his parallel intellectual intentions of disruption and reinvention. Perhaps his reworking of the sonnet form is another attempt to understand Cromwell more deeply by immersing himself in the common literary forms with which Cromwell would have been familiar while simultaneously locating the poetic voice in the prime catalytic environment of the knowledgeable and dangerous insider. If, as Roy Foster claims, the Elizabethan English believed that "Irish nationality had to be uprooted by the sword" (Foster, 1988: 8), then Kennelly's abundant use of the sonnet as a form of inquiry in his poems marks a moment of reappropriation and reconfiguration of the influence of the crucial Elizabethan era on the development of models of the Irish nation and its literature. The sonnet is now Buffun's tool, as much the articulation of the occupied as the occupier, and through its usage Kennelly can begin to exorcise the ghost of the literary form which was used by many influential figures to define the colonised Irish. Buffun's liking of the sonnet now becomes concurrently more understandable in the light of his search for self-identity. In "Master", Kennelly uses another voice, that of Edmund Spenser, to slyly indicate his intentions and he points to the significance of his own choice of the sonnet as the prime vehicle in his epic sequence:

> "As relief from my Queene, I write sonnets
> But even these little things get out of hand
> Now and then, giving me a nightmare head.
> Trouble is, sonnets are genetic epics.
> Something in them wants to grow out of bounds.
> I'm up to my bollox in sonnets" Spenser said. (*C*, 81)

In the note to *Cromwell*, Kennelly states that "this poem tries to present the nature and implications of various forms of dream and nightmare, including the nightmare of Irish history" (*C*, 5) and his choice of a dream sequence as a poetic vehicle is a significant and influential factor in the effectiveness of the poems. Buffun's imagination is the arena in which the competing voices of the past and the present do battle in an "imagistic" (*C*, 6) sequence of poems that deal with what Kennelly refers to as "connection and disconnection, with inevitable attitudes of condescension and servility, exploitation and retaliation, cultivation and neglect, in the historical/political world" (*ATFV*, 13). Buffun experiences these connections in his dreams when his subconscious mind gives way to all the forces at play behind his waking memory. Consequently, Buffun's experience of his personal maturation is enhanced by the totality of images that are liberated in his dreams. Whatever forces — historical, familial or sexual — are sublimated by his conscious mind now seek a frantic and vital expression in the cauldron of his subconscious existence.

Buffun's dreams closely parallel the necessary maturation that a postcolonial country must undergo if the colonial experience is to be assimilated into contemporary models of national identity, and through the persona of Buffun, Kennelly posits the opinion that models of nationhood are largely composed of undigested phantasmagoria which are used to feed politically and socially loaded concepts of the nation. Buffun's dreams provide a vehicle for the expression and deconstruction of crucial cultural signifiers, popular composite elements on the essentially ephemeral concept of the nation. Indeed, his dreams allow all the prejudices and phobias that constitute his being to surface in an honest reappraisal of self, a process that is mirrored in the national search for identity. His dreams cannot be discounted and have to be confronted in a difficult and painful process of self-examination and self-criticism.

In his seminal work *The Interpretation of Dreams*, Sigmund Freud claims that "all the material making up the content of a dream is in some way derived from experience" (Freud, 1954: 11), a claim that validates the often surreal and brutal dreams that Buffun experiences. He cannot of course have met Oliver Cromwell, as he lives in contemporary times, but has been taught to hate him to such a degree that this hate has entered his waking memory, principally in childhood. Consequently, in his dreams, Buffun engages not only with Cromwell but with the dominant formative influences in his life, many of which he may have forgotten in his waking memory but who are given free expressive reign in his dreams. Kennelly attempts to articulate what Freud refers to as the "dream-imagination" (Freud, 1954: 84), a state of extreme liberation for Buffun in which his often restrained imagination "leaps into a position of unlimited sovereignty" (Freud, 1954: 84), free from the control of his waking reason.

In fact, Freud's analysis of the dream-imagination provides a valuable framework within which Buffun's dreams become self-explanatory. Freud argues that:

> though dream-imagination makes use of recent waking memories for its building material, it erects them

into structures bearing not the remotest resemblance
to those of waking life; it reveals itself in dreams as
possessing not merely reproductive but productive
powers. (Freud, 1954: 84)

Thus Buffun's various absurd images of Oliver Cromwell op-
erating a taxi business in Kerry, Edmund Spenser as an alco-
holic auctioneer and William of Orange as a furniture
polisher (*C,* 151) become plausible contemporary connections
between the past and the present. Indeed, these connections
are a key manifestation of the influence of history on con-
temporary existence in that imagined characteristics inherent
in the historical figure become realised in the contemporary
representation of distinctive national stereotypes. The char-
acteristics Buffun experiences in those around him, and the
national characteristics he is exposed to, elicit the connec-
tions with Cromwell and others in his dream-imagination.

Two crucial questions now arise: if an individual can have
such a vibrant personal dream-imagination, could a collective
national dream-imagination also exist? To what degree do
images and icons of nationhood exist in such a collective na-
tional dream-imagination? While Freud does not directly deal
with these questions, it is central to understanding the effec-
tiveness of *Cromwell* as a unified text because Kennelly en-
gages precisely in Freud's description of the processes of the
dream-imagination:

It [dream-imagination] shows a preference for what is
immoderate, exaggerated and monstrous. But at the
same time, being freed from the hindrances of the
categories of thought, it gains in pliancy, agility and
versatility. (Freud, 1954: 84)

Buffun's dreams are certainly pliant, agile and versatile in their
approach to and treatment of history. The supposed demons
of Irish history, from Oliver Cromwell to William of Orange,

are themselves freed by Buffun's dream-imagination into an environment where they can express opinions suppressed in the national waking memory because they clash with the dominant perception of national identity. Buffun too is free to challenge or accept whatever version he pleases as he has been liberated from his respective reason-bound existence. Kennelly allows a crucial debate over Irish national identity to take place in Buffun's dreams, a debate that ranges over, amongst other crucial national signifiers, the role of language, history and religion in the colonial and postcolonial eras. However, Buffun's dreams also portray the immoderate, exaggerated and monstrous constructions contained within the dream-imagination. The abstract nature of many of his dreams feed into his search for a more valid and disparate model of identity. Buffun, and Kennelly, are both searching for those crucial nodal points of connection between competing histories and interpretations.

His personal identity, in parallel with the national identity, is composed of many disparate internal voices and personalities, each contributing to what Freud refers to as "external plastic pictures" (Freud, 1954: 84), composite icons of identity that are based on internal intellectual and imaginative constructions. It is these "external plastic pictures", artificial and pliant, that form the images and icons of nationhood and it is through this epic examination of the dream-imagination that a vital and creative deconstruction and revaluation of both the self and the nation can take place. Indeed, these Freudian pictures are seminal composite elements in the construction of national myths, most of which Kennelly seeks to deconstruct in the course of the collection. In this way, *Cromwell* can be viewed as an excellent literary example of the theories outlined by Benedict Anderson, Homi K. Bhabha, Colin Graham, and others who seek to analyse the unstable and often illusory nature of both individual and collective national identities. Specifically, *Cromwell* addresses Anderson's notion of "ghostly national imaginings" (Anderson, 1983: 9) by thoroughly examining a historical figure who was crucial in the formation of a popular version of Irish identity. Anderson argues that the process of deconstructing the edifice of a fixed perception of national identity must involve a painful exorcism similar to that experienced by Buffun. One of the poem's great successes is its very engagement with a formative "national imagining", personified in the figure of Oliver Cromwell. The latter's interaction with Buffun highlights the realisation that national identity is a far more complex and inter-related matter which requires careful and honest self-scrutiny. The poem puts revealing flesh on the ghost of a man whose reputation helped galvanise a perception of identity fuelled by hatred and fear.

The poem occupies what Homi K. Bhabha refers to as an "innovative site of collaboration and contestation" (Bhabha, 1994, 1–2) because it refuses to be delimited by the overwhelming discourses of nationalist or unionist histories by existing on the crucial boundaries of self and national identity. Similarly, Colin Graham asserts that postcolonial theory must examine the "liminal spaces" (Graham, 1994: 29) that occupy the edges of perceptions of national identity, an assertion that has parallels in Bhabha's work. Graham also argues that "there is no Irish cultural criticism which questions both the nature of and the underlying necessities for Irishness as a category" (private correspondence, 3 March 1997) yet in *Cromwell* there certainly appear to be the stirrings of just such a questioning debate.

This hermeneutic of categorical suspicion is central to the overall critical effectiveness of the collection. While Cromwell is a character who appears relatively secure in his personal, religious and national identities, Buffun is afforded no such security. His very Irishness appears as an accidental consequence of his birth, his personal characteristics a matter of universal experience rather than directly forged in a unique cultural setting. The collection continually seeks to portray

Buffun as a troubled, postmodern Everyman, a man for whom home is a place that is constantly "shifting" or occasionally "glimpsed" as an amalgam of mud and water (*C*, 158). In "Home", the third-last poem in the collection, Buffun casually notes that what he calls home is a "strange territory" (*C*, 158), the anonymous moniker resolutely distancing itself from an Irish context into the more collectively experienced difficulties of defining the essence of the national space. Buffun is content in his isolation, whatever liberation he feels at the end of his troubled dialogue with Cromwell tentatively emerging as an acknowledgement of the artificial nature of all that is labelled Irish. He refers to himself as an "emigrant" whose country exists merely as a "parody" in his brain, while outwardly admitting that he likes "to whine about identity" and to "bullshit about being free" (*C*, 158). Thus the specifically Irish contexts of the poems, though important in themselves, consequently also serve as a backdrop to the modern questions of nationalism and national identity.

The crucial debate concerning the nature and consequences of linguistic colonisation in Ireland forms the basis of one of Buffun and Cromwell's many dialogues and, as with so many of the internal debates within the poem, Kennelly identifies the multiplicity of responses that linguistic displacement can elicit without polemically authenticating one particular position. He simultaneously highlights the postcolonial angst over relative linguistic authenticity and explores the ensuing possible conflicts and resolutions. In his dream-imagination, for example, Buffun is visited by a "1,000 year old soldier" (*C*, 39) who has "fond memories of looting and rape". He acknowledges his role in the destruction of the native language he encountered in the course of his military career:

> "Yes, I throttled words in many a throat
> And saw the blood boiling in their eyes
> When they stared into the face of silence.

I've witnessed this for centuries. Not
A pretty sight. But out of it, for you, this
Language I bring. Blood born, for your convenience." (*C*, 39)

Kennelly's ubiquitous soldier personifies the physical and cultural violence involved in linguistic colonisation. The almost inevitable outcome of the conflict between the language of the coloniser and the colonised is the initial domination of the coloniser's language by military force. This process is then underpinned by consequent social, cultural and educational practices designed to ensure that native languages, in Ngugi Wa Thiong'o's words, "were associated with negative qualities of backwardness, underdevelopment, humiliation and punishment" (Ngugi, 1986: pp. 15–16). David Lloyd, in his book *Anomalous States*, notes the dilemma that lies at the heart not only of the Irish situation but of any colonial situation when he identifies two presuppositions that underpin the notion of the linguistic deprivation of the native Irish in the face of the inevitable and unstoppable advance of English:

> The notion of linguistic deprivation depends, amongst other things, on two precepts which are already loaded in the colonial situation, namely, that the only authentic language of expression, for individual or nation, is the mother tongue and that, correlatively, expression of whatever in a second language will inevitably be inauthentic, deracinated, lame. On such a basis, the hybridity of Irish English, until it is refined into a literary medium of expression with its own regularities, can be seen only as signs of cultural damage rather than as indices of versatility. (Lloyd, 1993: 30)

Kennelly explores these critical national dilemmas in *Cromwell* and he concentrates on the complex and often dualistic responses hinted at by Lloyd. Poems such as "A Language" (*C*, 39) and "Someone, Somewhere" (*C*, 41) portray the profound sense of loss that can accompany linguistic colonisation, however difficult such a loss is to define. The voice in "A Language" laments the passing of stories, folk-tales, place-names, local histories and other important cultural signifiers with the arrival of the colonial language and the strong inference is the crucial role of the representativeness of language in the formation of local and national identities. The representative nature of language lies at the heart of differing interpretations of the consequences of linguistic colonisation and an examination of its representative value will throw valuable light on Kennelly's interpretation of the function of language. Edward Said poses the critical question in *Orientalism*:

> The real issue is whether indeed there can be a true representation of anything, or whether any and all representations, because they are representations, are embedded first in the language and then in the culture, institutions and political ambience of the representer. If the latter alternative is the correct one (as I believe it is), then we must be prepared to accept the fact that a representation is *eo ipso* implicated, intertwined, embedded, interwoven with a great many other things besides the "truth", which is itself a representation. (Said, 1991: 272)

Said locates language at what Kennelly refers to as a crucial point of "connection" (*ATFV*, 12) and he argues that any representations of nationhood are inevitably bound up with the language of the representer. The inherent difficulty in the colonial situation is the conflict between the linguistic representations of the coloniser and the colonised, both of whom seek that elusive quality of authenticity, while language itself becomes representative of political and cultural interests rather than a mere means of communication. Said argues that representations are "interwoven with a great many other things", a proposition that highlights the dangers of linguistic reductionism in the colonial and postcolonial eras. *Cromwell* illuminates many of Said's impinging factors, such as economics, education, history, social class and cultural fashions, forces that conspire to shape linguistic preferences and consequently models of nationhood.

Declan Kiberd has noted that in the first decades of the Irish Free State there existed "a pet theory that Irishness was only to be found in the Gaelic tradition" (Kiberd, 1995: 555), an observation that points to the divisive nature of linguistic representation in the Irish postcolonial context. The concurrent attempt to deny the existence and cultural validity of a vibrant Irish English no doubt contributed to the draconian censorship laws of the early decades of the Free State and the ironic situation described by Kiberd:

> If nineteenth-century critics in England had a full-time job stripping Shakespeare and other writers of their radical potentials, the academics of twentieth-century Ireland devoted themselves with equal solicitude to the deradicalisation of native writing in both languages. (Kiberd, 1995: 561)

The potentially damaging consequences of such a policy have been clearly outlined by Ngugi:

> It [colonial alienation] starts with a deliberate dissociation of the language of conceptualisation, of thinking, of formal education, of mental development, from the language of daily interaction in the home and community. It is like separating the mind from the body so that they are occupying two unrelated spheres in the same person. (Ngugi, 28)

While Ngugi's model has obvious chronological differences from the Irish experience, the long-term consequences of this alienation of language from community is one of the themes explored in *Cromwell*. Ngugi's sense of alienation in

Kenya is raw and contemporary, while the Irish experience of linguistic dislocation spans a far longer period and the sense of alienation, it could be argued, is at a more complex and dualistic stage, yet none the less palpable. Indeed, Kennelly has translated some of the most important early Irish poems and his interest in the old Irish form is attested to by his 1989 book *Love of Ireland: Poems from the Irish*, which includes versions of, amongst others, "The Old Woman of Beare", "Blackbird" and "Etain". Kennelly's bilingualism certainly elicits a deal of cross-fertilisation that is clearly noticeable in both the form and rhythm of his poems and the shorter translations in this collection compare favourably with Kennelly's more recent reworking of Martial's epigrams.

Throughout *Cromwell*, Kennelly attempts to articulate a variety of representers, voices that occasionally stand in direct opposition, in order to elicit the multivalent hybridity and complex structure of the postcolonial linguistic condition. He has written that "it does no harm to feel homeless in a language", a perspective that forces a climate of self-analysis in which "the problem is to be at home in the sense of homelessness" (Kennelly, 1994: 70). His feeling of homelessness, however, is not an acknowledgement of rootlessness, but rather an appreciation of a linguistic inheritance whose value lies, in Homi K. Bhabha's words, "in displaying the wide dissemination through which we construct the field of meanings and symbols associated with national life" (Bhabha, 1990: 3). He does this by allowing the various responses to linguistic colonisation a freedom of expression in Buffun's dream-imagination, ranging from the pragmatic and utilitarian acceptance of English in the neo-colonial economic era to the personal and national identity crisis initiated by the loss of a native linguistic representation. In the poem "What Use?", a voice expresses virtual contempt for Irish in the face of the economic necessity of emigration to Britain. The voice asks Buffun:

"Can you see me facing a foreman in England
Equipped with my native sounds, asking for a start
To prove I can use my hands
Like any other man from any other land?
That language should have been strangled at birth
To stop it wasting my heart and mind." (*C*, 40)

This voice could easily represent any one of the 500,000 people who emigrated from Ireland between 1946 and 1961 (Cairns and Richards, 1988: 13), thus escaping a stagnant and hypocritical Irish society bitterly attacked by Sean O'Faolain, Frank O'Connor and Patrick Kavanagh, amongst others. The voice in "What Use?" questions the motivations behind successive government policies that paid lip-service to the ideal of an Irish-speaking Ireland while tacitly allowing the old colonial power to shore up the "central vacuity" (Cairns and Richards, 1988: 139) at the heart of Irish life. There is a deep anger expressed towards the Irish language in "What Use?", reflective perhaps of the isolation of the Irish language by the Free State government as the prime cultural restorative tool in the postcolonial era, regardless of the massive social, cultural and economic consequences of large-scale emigration. This anger appears to be clearly aimed at those who have used it for nationalistic ends, in that the pragmatic benefits of English, which allow the speaker an economic parity "with any other man from any other land", are compared to the implied image of a language as a sick, incubated baby, artificially kept alive for some archaic, ill-defined purpose. In his book *Inventing Ireland*, Declan Kiberd accuses the Free State education system of producing, "with dire predictability, a people lacking in self-confidence and easily bullied by outsiders" (Kiberd, 1995: 553) and the attitude expressed towards Irish in Kennelly's poem reflects the inherent difficulties of attaching sole importance to language as the saviour of national identity.

The voice refers to the Irish language "wasting my heart and mind", reinforcing the impression of the isolation of language revival from key economic and social policies. It could be argued that this was ultimately counter-productive in that Irish, because it was not directly linked to job-creation schemes and other regenerative social, economic and cultural policies, became associated with the causal factors of widespread emigration. The native language, therefore, rather than eliciting crucial cultural responses in the hearts of the people, becomes a postcolonial millstone, its revival a political shibboleth to disguise the paucity of imagination and leadership that gripped the Free State in its early decades. In this poem, Kennelly depicts possibly hundreds of thousands of people labouring in the building sites of the former colonial power, accepting both the colonial language and the wage it offers, conveniently ignored by an Irish government unable to provide an economic future for its citizens while promoting an archaic language that no longer reflects practical realities.

While the postcolonial authorities bear an element of responsibility for this particular situation, Ngugi identifies the response of the voice in poems like "What Use?" as a direct consequence of the "cultural bomb", a devastating legacy of both colonialism and imperialism designed to ensure that the process of alienation continues even after the colonial era has come to an end. The effect of this cultural bomb is

> . . . to annihilate a people's belief in their names, in their languages, in their environment, in their heritage of struggle, in their unity, in their capacities and ultimately in themselves. It makes them see their past as one wasteland of non-achievement and it makes them want to distance themselves from that non-achievement. It makes them want to identify with that which is furthest removed from their own; for instance, with other people's languages rather than their own. (Ngugi, 1986: 3)

This description closely parallels the opinions expressed in "What Use?" concerning the efficacy of the Irish language. While "that damned language" is associated with unemployment and social and personal humiliation, English presents itself as the saviour language, "blood-born, for your convenience" (*C*, 39), facilitating economic survival and advancement, thereby guaranteeing its position in the linguistic character of the country. The longer this situation persists, the more the cultural bomb begins to infiltrate the psyche of the people to the degree that the native language becomes increasingly marginalised and its survival becomes dependant upon the financial support of governments and the intellectual credibility of a linguistic minority.

This linguistic pragmatism is, of course, just one possible response to Ngugi's "cultural bomb". The loss of the daily significance of a native language concurrently signals a crucial and definitive shift in the cultural, social and political development of a country and contributes significantly to the process of cultural and political colonisation. In the postcolonial era, Edward Said points out that along with a reappropriation of the land by native people, a central cultural touchstone involves "an almost magically inspired, quasi-alchemical- redevelopment of the native language" (Said, 1993:, 273), a process that another voice in Buffun's dream-imagination attempts to articulate in the Irish context. Interestingly, Kennelly places "Someone, Somewhere" as the next poem after "What Use?", thus physically juxtaposing these two conflicting perspectives. The voice in "Someone, Somewhere" states categorically that "I do not believe this language is dead" (*C*, 41) and "So long as I live my language will live", thus closely allying the native language with perceptions of self, a position directly dismissed in "What Use?". The voice condemns the pragmatist for believing the colonial "lie":

"No, of course you don't hear me, why should you,
You who believe what has always been said,
Let us bury our language, our language is dead." (C, 41)

However, the desire for linguistic renewal contained in this poem differs from the politically inspired attempts of the Free State governments to renew Irish while maintaining the basics of colonial education practices and syllabi. This voice is closer to Said's "almost magically inspired, quasi-alchemical" model of linguistic renewal, vowing to engage physically in the process of restoration in Martin Luther King-type rhetoric:

"I have a notion, I have a bike
And I'm going to ride it through the back roads
Of Ireland. Each road, in its turn,
Will twist me to people, my people, whose minds
Will dance to those words buried
In their hearts. Someone, somewhere, will learn." (C, 41)

The voice makes no reference to the economic advantages of English but points to the personal joy and self-knowledge that would spring from a renewal of the native language, combining both the intellectual and emotional renaissance that would ensue. The emphasis on "my people" hints at the unifying properties of a native language, a cultural signifier that carries with it the germ of resistance to the colonial onslaught. Indeed, this introspection echoes Eamon de Valera's well-known St Patrick's Day address of 1943 in which, interestingly, he referred to "that Ireland which we dreamed of" (Moynihan, 1980: 446) as a site of elysian cultural and national purity. Both Kennelly and de Valera, therefore, appear to advocate the dream-imagination as the site for all kinds of revivals, linguistic, national and cultural, relishing an elastic nirvana in which debates can flow and where all sorts of potential outcomes can be articulated. The voice's bike ride through the back roads of Ireland is also reminiscent of W.B. Yeats and Douglas Hyde's search for the essential Celtic character, the former in the villages of Sligo and the latter in the cottages of Roscommon. Kennelly's voice chooses the back roads in its search for those who will revitalise the language, suggesting an Irish equivalent of Terry Eagleton's definition of "Englishness", at the start of the twentieth century, as "rural, populist and provincial rather than metropolitan and aristocratic" (Eagleton, 1983: 145). This voice believes in the restorative cultural powers of language and determines quietly to seek out those who will join in the restorative programme, certain in the knowledge that "someone, somewhere" will learn.

Kennelly appears deliberately to choose voices from the extreme ends of the linguistic debate, ignoring those voices representing the middle ground in favour of the polarised voices at the ends of the cultural spectrum. This practice obviously brings the debate into a clearer focus but perhaps fails to acknowledge, or at least articulate, the confused, questioning middle ground of those caught between a pragmatic acceptance of English and a sense of loss over the decline of Irish. "What Use?" and "Someone, Somewhere" highlight the polarisation that can occur in any cultural debate and are typical of Kennelly's analytical style. He has written that through poetry "we are brought into closer, more articulate contact with fiercely energetic forces which are at work within and outside ourselves" (Kennelly, 1994: 44). and it is perhaps this drive to understand these forces that leads him to focus on the extremities.

Ultimately, Kennelly does not presume to offer a solution to the linguistic dilemma of the relative authenticity, practicality and cultural significance of the two languages. Oliver Cromwell, on the other hand, is in no doubt as to his role in the imposition of English as the colonial and ultimately dominant and beneficial language of Ireland. He informs Buffun that "your native tongue strikes me as barbarous" (*C*, 45) and "If the people of England are the people of God / Then England's language is the language of heaven" (*C*, 45). His advice to Buffun is to study English carefully in order to "universalise your views" (*C*, 45), advice that echoes Chinua Achebe's declaration in 1964 that "I have been given a language [English] and I intend to use it" (quoted in Ngugi, 1986: 7). Cromwell tells Buffun that "I will be remembered as a killer of language" (*C*, 104) echoes the soldier's admission that "I throttled words in many a throat" (*C*, 39). These images of the violence involved in linguistic colonisation occur frequently in Buffun's dream-imagination, personified by a skulking wolf that "plays with the toy of my sleep" (*C*, 48), echoing "Dream of a Black Fox" in which Kennelly's imagination is stalked by an imaginary yet palpable dream fear. The wolf represents the culmination of Buffun's nightmares, forcing him into an admission of the self-doubt and uncertainty that lies at the heart of his linguistic questioning and his intense questioning goes beyond a mere intellectual exercise into the realms of his very being:

> While he makes me doubt all that I am and am
> Not, seized by the milling syllables of my name (*C*, 48)

The focus of Buffun's doubt is "the milling syllables" of his name. His name is, in fact, a hybrid construction, a clever linguistic combination of Irish and English, as Kennelly has written: "the name itself is half-Irish, u fada, and half-English — Buff, re-buff" (private correspondence, 1 April 1996). Perhaps Kennelly is hinting at the essential quality of hybridity that exists in all languages, as indeed it must exist in all concepts of a nation. Buffun is a hybrid, his English name closely paralleling the word "buffoon", pointing perhaps to an Irish equivalent of *King Lear*'s Fool, being, according to Kennelly, "dangerous when he's accepted as the fool" (private correspondence, 1 April 1996). Kennelly has also pointed to the word "rebuff" as a constituent of Buffun's name, because through his dream imagination, Buffun rejects the labels and clichés placed upon his personal and national identity by involuntarily exploring the complex forces that have conspired to shape his identity. "Buffun knows what Buffun knows, but may conceal it" (private correspondence, 1 April 1996) and this is a clear hint from Kennelly that Buffun is a stronger person for his nightmarish experiences in that he is engaged in a process of questioning and self-exploration, seeking the origins of his hybridity, exemplified by his name, and in the process arriving at the precarious yet ultimately liberating position of being at home in a sense of homelessness. Indeed, Buffun's personal odyssey extends to other areas that have impacted upon his psyche, and his dialogues with Cromwell over the religious imperatives in the latter's Irish campaigns form the basis of another of their interactions, with Cromwell setting the tone in the sonnet "Praise the Lord":

> "Let's get one thing clear", said Oliver, "One thing alone:
> My life's purpose is to praise the lord
> Whatever I have suffered, wherever I have gone,
> No matter when or where I have warred
> Against The Enemy, the hand
> Of The Lord has always worked for me.
> I saw Heaven's lightning descend on England
> And burn up idle bluster in a night.
>
> If I conducted a terrible Surgery
> On some, I pity them. They are pitiable enough.
> Yet The Lord's hand guided me right.
> Whenever I killed, I killed from His love,
> His hand in mine, His ways my ways.
> For all I've done, I tender Him all praise." (*C*, 83)

Thus, in a poem strongly reminiscent of his earlier "Oliver Cromwell Looks at an Irish Actor Playing the Part of Oliver Cromwell", Cromwell informs Buffun not only of his personal religious zeal but the lengths to which he is prepared to go to ensure that his interpretation of the Lord's work is carried out. This is a central and repeated justification for Cromwell throughout the poem and he genuinely appears to believe in the righteousness of his cause in Ireland. Kennelly uses Cromwell's almost unshakeable belief in his divinely inspired task to explore the nature and function of the Catholic and Protestant religions in Ireland's colonial past and the consequences for the present. Cromwell's absolute belief in the legitimacy of his cause was reflected in the conduct of his soldiers:

> One reason why Cromwell's troopers fought superbly was that they believed they were fighting the Lord's battles. Many of their chaplains stood on the extreme left wing of puritanism, and instilled in them a faith that the overthrow of tyranny in church and state was only the first stage in the unfolding of God's great purpose for England. They saw themselves as the shock-troops of a chosen second people, and their goal was the New Jerusalem — the progressive realisation of the Kingdom of God on earth. (Woolrych, 1970: 61)

Cromwell brought this certitude to his Irish campaign and he repeatedly tells Buffun, most specifically in "An Expert Teacher" (*C*, 69), that he is nothing more than the executor of God's will, yet he does occasionally acknowledge his own role in the interpretation of this divine plan. Buffun does not engage Cromwell in a debate over the religious overtones in his military campaign and gradually the impression is created of a religious fanaticism dangerously allied to a political and military machine that results in an almost irresistible force. Cromwell uses terms such as "ordained" and "judgement" (*C*, 69) to reinforce his interpretation of the divine and inevitable nature of his violence in Ireland. The shedding of blood is in itself, for him, as with the Crusaders of the twelfth century, a cathartic experience. "Drowning, fire, strangling, sword and gun" (*C*, 69) are an inherent part of Cromwell's religious expression and not merely an unpleasant side-effect of completing the Lord's work. His soldiers approach the killing of children "with Herodean vigour" (*C*, 57), sure of the importance and righteousness of their work. John Morrill argues that Cromwell's personal troubles during the period 1629–31, what he describes as his "dark night of the soul", was a formative influence in his interpretation of the purpose of suffering. He notes:

> Cromwell's view of God's plan for England was to remain malleable and ever-changing. But his knowledge that God had a plan for England and that he was a part of that plan sustained him through war in three kingdoms and through a political career that brought him via regicide to the very edge of the throne itself. The personal faith of the man who was to be Lord Protector of England, Scotland and Ireland had been forged in the crucible of a deep personal crisis. (Morrill, 1993: 147)

Thus there can be little doubt as to the sincerity of Cromwell's religious zeal and this fact is attested to by Kennelly in poems such as "Oliver Writes to the Speaker of the Parliament of England" (*C*, 55), "Oliver to a Friend" (*C*, 118) and "Oliver on Fear and Love" (*C*, 102). In these poems, however, there are elements of the ironic detachment that is a feature of Kennelly's implied criticism of ideological reductionism in the rest of the collection. Indeed, the ironic treatment of important themes is a hugely effective poetic device and Kennelly uses this ironic detachment to observe critically the environments in which his respective protagonists operate. Cromwell's religious zeal emerges as a driving force behind his actions, a sincerely held belief in the validity and sanctity of those actions, but he is singularly incapable of appreciating the brutal, dehumanising and in many ways anti-Christian consequences of his beliefs. What is most disquieting about Cromwell's beliefs is the fact that he recognises that the natural result of his interpretation of God's plan will involve the killing of those who stand in the way of the implementation of that plan. His faith has dehumanised him to the extent that he cannot subjectify the brutality being meted out by his soldiers, particularly on the residents of Drogheda. This is where Kennelly allows Cromwell to be seen, in the more objective light of Buffun's imagination, as a determined, bigoted and brutal persecutor, rather than as the Lord Protector he wished to be known as. Cromwell cannot see the huge contradictions inherent in his religion, where his fierce anti-Catholicism fuels his Irish campaign, and it is a situation parodied by Kennelly in "Friends" (*C*, 97):

> Jesus is Oliver's friend, they get on well
> Together despite the occasional
> Tiff concerning the nature of pain
> Inflicted on folk who lack the cop-on
> To comply with Oliver's ironside commands.

In many ways, Cromwell stands accused of the very criticism he lays at contemporary Ireland in the cuttingly apposite "Therefore, I Smile" (*C*, 150) when he argues that his memory was "an excuse for what they would fail to do", his memory being composed of "twisted poems and stories". Cromwell gives Jesus a voice and uses him to justify his activities. Jesus certainly has "tendered them the terrible gift of my name" (*C*, 150) and many thousands of people are killed by Cromwell and his soldiers in the name of Jesus. If contemporary Ireland is unable to see Oliver Cromwell as anything other than the brutal epitome of English barbarism, then Cromwell is unable to see Jesus as anything other than a justification for the violence inflicted upon his political enemies. Perhaps Kennelly is pointing to the cyclical and repetitive

nature of historical reductionism where each era utilises fig-
ures from the past to justify untenable positions and where
the past is raided to yield a tailored version of the "truth".
Kennelly is paralleling two central figures in Irish cultural his-
tory, separated both by time and space, but both having an
enormous contemporary influence on the colonial and post-
colonial models of Irish nationhood. Cromwell uses Jesus in
much the same way as Ireland uses Cromwell, namely as a
convenient and powerful symbol of an ideology that seeks
validity through the voiceless — though, obviously, from op-
posite perspectives: Jesus being a heroic figure (in epic
terms), Cromwell being the villain. Kennelly's Cromwell
serves the purpose of deflecting attention away from more
tangible causes of contemporary problems while Cromwell
himself utilises Jesus to exonerate himself and his troops from
any charges of brutality. Kennelly appears to suggest that
both Cromwell and Jesus serve a dangerous and interactive
purpose, that of a malleable, manipulative focus for preju-
dices, bigotries and ultimately violence. Kennelly is already
attempting in *Cromwell* what he explicitly intended in the Pref-
ace to *The Book of Judas* in 1991:

> When one tries to substitute the uncertainties of al-
> truistic exploration for the certainties of inherited
> hate, one is immediately disrupting and challenging
> one's "cultural legacy", spitting in the faces of the au-
> thoritative fathers and their revered, unimpeachable
> wisdom. The process of unlearning hate is a genuine
> insult to some, particularly those whose prejudices
> are called convictions. (*J*, 9)

While Cromwell's religious bigotry and violence are ex-
plored in the poem, Kennelly also explores the much less dis-
cussed violence meted out by Catholics against Protestants
over the course of Ireland's colonial history. The anti-
Protestant nature of many of the poems hints at a deeper

feeling than mere revenge for the violence inflicted by Cromwell on the Catholic population of Ireland and points towards the popularly held conviction that Irish Protestants were one step removed from the authentic Irish psyche while the close link between Irishness and Catholicism echoes Cromwell's image of God's plan for England and his notion that England "Is an emblem of Heaven" (*C*, 68).

Indeed, the level of violence on both sides is a feature of many of the poems and Kennelly appears to be pointing towards the futile and barbarous nature of religious expression in Ireland where violence, be it physical or mental, appears to be its defining characteristic. This is, of course, highly relevant to the violence associated with the "Troubles" in the north of Ireland, a fact attested to by the inclusion of the poem "Nails" (*C*, 135), in which a van packed with nails explodes beside a group of unsuspecting schoolchildren. The ubiquitous nature of violence in Irish life is strongly implied when the narrator notes that "these blasted crucifixes are commonplace" (*C*, 135), while the exploding van bridges the chronological gap between the child-killers of the North and "Oliver's boys" (*C*, 57) approaching the task of the killing of children with "Herodean vigour" (*C*, 57). One rebel soldier, in the poem "A Holy War" (*C*, 62) describes the ripping open of pregnant women's stomachs in order that "little lords" might not escape their due in what he describes as "a holy war" while less heavily pregnant women were buried alive under piles of stones or piked to death. The justification given is the holy nature of the war and the staunch defence of the Catholic faith and its spiritual leader, the Pope, by Catholic rebels. Predictably, the Catholic response to religious violence is almost identical in tone and deed to its Protestant counterpart, the Protestant religion being regarded as the essential manifestation of English colonial intent. The "big important Protestant house" (*C*, 58) becomes the focus of seething Catholic hatred, the residents stripped and burned and some hung, drawn and quartered in public. This abject violence directed at the big house develops the threats issued in an earlier poem that dealt with the consequences of colonisation, namely "Statement of the Former Occupant" from *The House That Jack Didn't Build*. The former occupant warns Jack that there will be a cost involved in his enforced eviction:

> Don't be disturbed
> If you see me skulking
> Near your house that was once my house
> And may be my house again. (*HJDB*, 14)

Protestant corpses are dug up ("Do Good" (*C*, 60)) and "half-hanging" (*C*, 60) becomes the rebels' favoured treatment of Protestant prisoners. The unnamed Catholic in the poem "The Cause" (*C*, 73) notes that God "orders us to burn all their houses", and "all that we do is for religion", a phrase that strongly echoes Cromwell's words when he states that "whenever I killed, I killed from his love" (*C*, 83). Thus juxtaposed, a resolution to this conflict appears virtually impossible. God is the supporter of both causes and the justification for horrific and sadistic violence. Both Catholics and Protestants intone the same images of God and use virtually the same language to condemn each other, applying hollow labels to signify a perceived fundamental difference.

While the crucial social, cultural and political role of religion in Ireland's colonial past and postcolonial present is manifested in *Cromwell* mainly through the graphic account of the violence handed out by Protestants on Catholics and vice versa, these extremes point to a more complex religious debate with which Buffun appears reluctant to engage. His dream-imagination is bombarded by violent images which appear precisely at moments when Buffun attempts to reflect more deeply on the consequences of his religious history and legacy. In "Mass Rock" (*C*, 151), for example, Buffun stumbles towards a mass rock (an unofficial site for mass, usually a prominent local stone or rock, used primarily after the establishment of the penal laws in 1704), acknowledging that neither he nor the souls who occupy his dream-imagination have ever known "peace", and he decides that in a place of solitude and reflection he will pray and attempt to understand the nature of his religious experiences. However, seated on top of the mass rock is a motley collection of cats "of every hue and breed" who declare to Buffun that "tonight it's certain some of us will bleed". Their rallying call is "Attack! Defend! Attack! Defend!" and consequently Buffun is denied the space and time to reflect on the peace that has passed him by. Religion is again depicted in a violent, militaristic series of images that deliberately avoid analysis and thrive on the brutality engendered by bigotry and ignorance. The consequences of this for Buffun are serious. He is unable to find any escape from the violence in his dream-imagination and as a result he becomes increasingly detached from the Catholic culture that dominates his environment. Religion, like language, becomes a source of unease and distress, another focus for the many hatreds that Buffun experiences at first hand in his dreams. The images of burnings, mutilations and killings carried out in the name of Christ induce Buffun into a state of freefall where he reels from the icons of religion, afraid of whatever atrocities awaits him in his dreams.

In "An Enlightened Man" (*C*,131), a Catholic priest tells his followers that there is no violence they cannot inflict on a Protestant that God would condemn and he goes so far as to suggest that Catholics were created by God for the very purpose of annihilating Protestants, a sentiment closely echoing Cromwell's attitude towards Catholics. Interestingly, the priest's name is Paddy Maguire, perhaps hinting at a connection with the protagonist of Patrick Kavanagh's 1942 epic poem *The Great Hunger*, a man who also experiences the largely negative nature of a brutalising Catholicism and who,

like Buffun, suffers a sense of alienation and isolation as a con-
sequence of the institutionalised church.

Buffun's religious experiences are not confined to his bru-
tal Cromwellian dreams although these dreams certainly form
a strong impression on his imagination. He also dreams of his
Confirmation Day in which he has a comical exchange with
the bishop:

> "What's peace?", he asks.
> "The ha-ha-harmony of the sus-sus-soul
> With Gug-Gug-God", I reply. "Beautiful", smiles the trout.
> (*C*, 47)

The reduction of complex religious and philosophical ideas
into the rote learning of a question-and-answer session points
to the institutionalised church's expectations of its followers
and it is a theme that can be found in many of Kennelly's ear-
lier poems, including "The Stick" and "Catechism". Buffun's
answers are nervously stammered out without any sense of
personal reflection or mature consideration on crucial per-
sonal developmental questions such as the nature of the rela-
tionship between self and soul. The bishop echoes
Cromwell's war-like brand of Christianity when he announces
that as a result of a series of stammered answers to learned
questions, Buffun "is now a soldier of Christ" (*C*, 47), appar-
ently equipped to take on an unnamed and unidentified foe.
This ceremony of confirmation would appear to corroborate
how little progress the religious debate has made in Ireland
since Cromwell's crusade and that the only consistent ele-
ment running through Buffun's religious experiences appears
to be violence, be it the obvious physical violence of the
Cromwellian era or the psychological violence of Buffun's
contemporary Catholic rites of passage. The function of this
exploration of the violence at the heart of Buffun's historical
and contemporary experience of religion is to heighten his

self-awareness and to force him into a crucial and revealing analysis of the forces that have shaped him into what he is.

Buffun cannot take his religion for granted because he is haunted by brutal and disturbing images of the damage caused in the name of religion. His exposition and witnessing of that violence enables him to more fully understand the origin of his own complex responses to religion and so that he can ironically begin tentatively to seek the peace that he so hopelessly and helplessly defined for the trout-faced bishop on his inappropriately named Confirmation Day. The deep wounds in Buffun's psyche that have been wrought by religion can only be cleaned and healed by a confrontation with the sources of that wounding.

At the end of the poems, however, Buffun is at the most difficult stage of recovery, namely that of the recognition of the problem. Kennelly has written of the importance of this confrontation:

> Reading becomes a kind of encounter with the repulsive, even the unspeakable. Returning from such encounters, we are more aware, more conscious. What we choose to do, or not to do, with our state of temporarily extended awareness, is our own affair. "Violent" poetry, the poetry of uncompromising consciousness, the poetry of hard, raw reality, continues to do its work of dramatic demonstration, of ruthless bringing to mind, of accusation and warning. This work is difficult, discomforting and increasingly necessary. (Kennelly, 1994: 44–5)

As with his reflections on the consequences of linguistic colonisation, neither Kennelly nor Buffun present an easy or circumscribed picture of Ireland's turbulent religious past or present. The overwhelmingly negative and often brutally violent images that occur in Buffun's dream-imagination attest to the difficult and oppositional nature of the conflict between the Catholic and Protestant traditions. Kennelly, however, is even-handed in portraying the brutality of both sides, thus blurring the distinction between the victim and the victimiser. The almost identical language, icons and behaviour of both Catholics and Protestants points to the common cultural inheritance of the two traditions and to a level of hatred that can only exist between those who have a deep knowledge and experience of the other. In this environment, religion, like language, becomes a convenient cultural marker of difference between the coloniser and the colonised and the adherence to a particular tradition becomes consequently more important as a mode of either domination or resistance. Buffun experiences the images of violence and repression and the result leaves him confused as to the nature of his personal religious composition. *Cromwell,* in Jonathan Allison's words, reflects "the Irish demonisation of Protestants and Englishmen which is the mirror-image of Cromwellian hatred of the Irish" (Pine, 1994: 88) and thus a self-perpetuating cycle is created in which religion becomes a focus for difference and intolerance. As with his linguistic dilemma, Buffun then moves from his religious interrogation to an engagement with the nature of historical hermeneutics in which, once again, a ferocious questioning is the norm. This exploration by Kennelly provides a poetic parallel to an earlier process identified by Roy Foster:

> By the 1960s the work of a whole generation of scholars had exploded the basis for popular assumptions about early Irish society, the conquest, the plantations, the eighteenth-century parliament, the record of landlordism, and most of all the continuities between the various forms of nationalism: in some cases, reverting to ideas held in the past by minority opinion but contemptuously dismissed. (Foster, 1993: 16)

Foster's analysis of the shift in Irish history away from a pious nationalism towards an iconoclastic revisionism provides an invaluable framework within which *Cromwell* and its critical significance can be more easily understood and it points to the wider context within which the poem deserves serious consideration. In his essay, "History and the Irish Question", Foster charts the move away from "simplistic historical hero-cults" and notes that "the Irish Sea has been re-interpreted as the centre, not the frontier, of a cultural area". *Cromwell* effectively portrays Irish history as a complex and non-reductive record of the interplay of competing forces and ideologies and Kennelly's brilliant chronological interstices serve as crucial contemporary correlatives. The process of history is primarily one of interpretation and Buffun's problems with history arise when he confronts the interpretations that have been forced upon him by virtue of his education and upbringing. The poem presents a version of Oliver Cromwell that jars, on occasion, with popular perceptions of the "Butcher of Drogheda", while the Lord Protector emerges from some of the poems as a caring father, a sincere Christian, a practical joker and confirmed democrat, aspects of his personality that have been largely ignored in the Irish nationalist canon. He also emerges, however, as a sexually perverted voyeur, his sexuality hovering on the edges of paedophilia and even necrophilia ("Honest-to-God Oliver" (*C*, 106) and "Performance" (*C*, 107)). He is unable to see the glaring contradictions in his character and it is here that Buffun strikes a blow for the revisionist and postcolonial view of history in that he is able to admit that "I spill my selves" (*C*, 159) while Cromwell can only picture his role in God's divine plan and is unable to see the moral and intellectual inadequacy of his position.

It is, of course, debatable whether Kennelly is providing a revised version of Oliver Cromwell and his role in Irish history or merely filling in the gaps in the overall picture of the historical figure. He is also seeking, perhaps, to correct an English caricature of the Puritan parliamentarian driven by righteous religious beliefs when Cromwell notes that "streets choked with rebel blood stimulate me" (*C*, 106) while he "revelled in wrecking and killing" (*C*, 87). This open admission of psychopathic violence is the correlative necessary in the debunking of the myth of the virtuous Lord Protector, as important in the English context as the tender epistles to his daughters are in the Irish context. Cromwell's violence is never denied or ignored and is, at times, almost overwhelming in its barbarity and depravity and Kennelly does not shrink from the responsibility of graphically portraying this side of his character. Indeed, there are times when Cromwell's overt pleasure in violence appears almost pathological and, while the poems indicting such tendencies are of course filtered through Buffun's imagination, Kennelly's list of sources in the note to *Cromwell* range from Christopher Hill to W.E.H. Lecky, suggesting a good deal of scholarly research to support such a picture. The massacre at Drogheda, for example, according to Roy Foster, "is one of the few massacres in Irish history fully attested to on both sides" (Foster, 1988: 102). Cromwell's tacit acknowledgment that the bloodshed at Drogheda was, in itself, a cause for "remorse and regret" (Abbott, 1939: 127), indicates a side to his personality that was rarely expressed over Irish affairs. He does not deny the barbarity of his soldiers' behaviour and records, in militaristic detail, the conquest of the town. His explanation of the exemplary nature of the violence and his often used phrase "to prevent the effusion of blood" appeared justified when both the towns of Trim and Dundalk quickly made peace with his advancing army. However, the severity of the violence cannot be avoided and even Cromwell admits to a certain regret, despite the fact that he claims, in the same breath, "that this is a righteous judgement of God". In her biography of Cromwell, Antonia Fraser has stated:

> The conclusion cannot be escaped that Cromwell lost
> his self-control at Drogheda, literally saw red — the
> red of his comrades' blood — after the failure of the
> first assaults, and was seized with one of those sudden
> brief and cataclysmic rages which would lead him to
> dissolve Parliament by force and sweep away that his-
> toric bauble. There were good militaristic reasons for
> behaving as he did, but they were not the motives
> which animated him at the time, during the day and
> night of uncalculated butchery. The slaughter itself
> stood quite outside his usual record of careful mercy
> as a soldier. (Fraser, 1973: 340)

Consequently, the demonising of Cromwell in Irish his-
tory relies principally, and it would appear fairly, on his repu-
tation for violence and this is confirmed in *Cromwell*. Kennelly
accepts this aspect of Cromwell's character as intrinsic to the
understanding of his overall impact on the Irish psyche, fash-
ioned as it is out of a cycle of repetitive sectarian violence. In
fact, in portraying the less violent and more sympathetic side
to Cromwell's personality, Kennelly actually emphasises the
brutality of Cromwell's Irish campaign because in his letters
to his daughter (*C*, 71), for example, he expresses a caring,
loving nature that wished the best for her future. In these
poems he is not a "butcher" but a doting and approachable
father whose sincere Christianity guides his actions. Rather
than debunking the myth of the Butcher, it could be argued
that Kennelly makes his violence all the more chilling and re-
pulsive because Cromwell was obviously capable of a loving
and understanding relationship with his daughters and others.
A pathological killer without remorse is, in many ways, easier
to understand than the schizophrenic actions of Oliver
Cromwell, a man capable of emotional extremes. Kennelly,
therefore, is engaged in a simultaneous process of revision
and confirmation of the historical figure by portraying both
the brutality and sentimentality of Oliver Cromwell. Crucially,

it is Cromwell himself who is allowed to justify his actions
and thus Kennelly attempts to offer an alternative reading of
what could be termed a national history.

Kennelly has developed this penchant for alternative his-
torical readings in subsequent collections. In *Begin* (1999),
Kennelly remembers Will Flint, a man he worked with on the
buses with in London in 1957. Flint had been a Black-and-Tan in
Cork during the Irish War of Independence (1919–21) and
Kennelly recalls a conversation:

> Having been reared
> to hate the thought
> of a Black-and-Tan
> the scum of England
> more beast than man
>
> I was somewhat surprised to find
> how much I liked Will Flint
> and his Black-and-Tan talk
> warming my heart and mind. (B, 68)

Flint talks of the "soft women of Buttevant" who "opened up
in style", suggesting a local complicity with the hated Black-
and-Tans, which is rarely if ever discussed in the pantheon of
Irish colonial resistance. Flint appears as an archetypal cock-
ney who was "'ardly a man" when he was sent to Ireland to
fight for "King and Country". He makes no apology for his
undoubtedly violent actions and innocently regards his bus-
driving job as a just reward for his service in Ireland. Much
like Oliver Cromwell's footsoldiers, Flint appears to be an
unwitting pawn in a larger plan, a young and gormless teen-
ager who went to Ireland on a form of adolescent adventure.
He does not appear to fit the bill of a ruthless, calculating
Black-and-Tan, hated by all the Irish people he came into con-
tact with. Resistance to his presence in Cork is certainly ac-
knowledged as he notes "I was lucky to get out alive" but in

typical Kennelly fashion the commonality of human experi-
ence is the over-riding emotion rather than polarised per-
spectives on fixed versions of history. Flint acts as a counter
to the demonisation of the Black-and-Tans in nationalist his-
toriography while also recognising the violence and brutality
for which he was partly responsible.

The central consequence of the function of history in
Cromwell is to emphasise the unstable and volatile nature of
history itself. History, in the Irish context, can so easily be-
come, in Cromwell's words, "echoing curses soaked in verbal
bile", full of "twisted stories" which become "an excuse for
what they would fail to do, to be, being themselves" (*C*, 150),
thus emphasising the notion of history as crutch. Notably, in
1971, F.S.L. Lyons appealed to historians for a historical revi-
sionism that found a clear and no doubt unexpected expres-
sion in the pages of *Cromwell*:

> The theories of revolution, the theories of nationality,
> the theories of history, which have brought Ireland to
> its present pass, cry out for re-examination and the
> time is ripe to try to break the great enchantment
> which for too long has made myth so much more
> congenial than reality. (Farrell, 1973: 223)

However, Oliver Cromwell cannot so easily exonerate
his role in the creation of these twisted stories and it is this
historical hermeneutical conundrum that concerns Kennelly
in *Cromwell*. In his analysis of Irish revolutionary movements
in the nineteenth and twentieth centuries, Tom Garvin notes:

> Republican separatist ideology was both modernising
> and nostalgic. Revolutionary imagery in many different
> societies has portrayed the desirable future in themes
> culled selectively from a real or imaginary past, com-
> bined with an equally selective set of images of the
> progressive future. The vision of the future depends
> on the vision of the past. (Garvin, 1987: 4)

This is a crucial point in the attempt to unravel the role of history in the construction of the icons and images of the Irish nation and also in the attempt to understand the nature and implications of Buffun's identity crisis. Of the entirety of Oliver Cromwell's fifty-nine years of life, only the ten months he spent in Ireland (from August 1649 to May 1650) are considered adequate in Irish nationalist historiography to construct an overall image of the essentially barbarous nature of his personality. This selective cull allows Cromwell to be demonised as the Butcher, despite historian Liam de Paor's comment that "in general his conduct of war compares not unfavourably with that of the late Elizabethan commanders" (de Paor, 1986: 168). Other prominent historians, such as J.C. Beckett, argue about the sack at Drogheda that "there seems to be no foundation for later stories of an indiscriminate slaughter of the whole civilian population" (Beckett, 1966: 102), opinions which crucially place Cromwell's violence in a larger context. In accordance with the rules of engagement, for example, Cromwell offered quarter to Sir Arthur Aston, the Governor of Drogheda, and wrote "If this is refused you will have no cause to blame me" (Abbott, 1939: 118). Aston refused to surrender and the attack began the next day. There is little doubt that Aston did indeed underestimate Cromwell's determination to crush Drogheda and therefore his culpability is a factor that has to be considered when assessing the massacre. It is in this larger context that Kennelly seeks to place Cromwell, pointing to the fact that Cromwell justified much of the violence as a simple retribution for the violence carried out by Catholics on Protestants in the 1641 rebellion (Foster, 1988: 85). Cromwell is certainly more guilty than many others involved in Ireland's bloody sectarian conflict, but there are others with blood on their hands who have escaped the demonisation inflicted upon him. *Cromwell*, according to Jonathan Allison, thus "avoids constructing the narrative of the Cromwellian campaign in simplistic moral terms, for the level of victimisation on every side is deep and unspeakably tragic" (Pine, 1994: 86).

The repetitive, cyclical nature of violence in Irish history permeates *Cromwell,* with the initial sectarian bloodshed of the Cromwellian era radiating into the Anglo-Irish war (1919–21), the outbreak of the troubles in the North and crystallising into specific acts such as the killing of Lord Mountbatten (see "Lettering" (*C,* 107)). There is a depressing predeterminism about much of the violence, each act of inhumanity being justified on the grounds of some other equally barbaric act of "the other side", usually Catholic against Protestant and vice versa, as Cromwell attests to in the poem "An Expert Teacher" (*C,* 69). Both sides then seek to sanction the violence through a process described by David Lloyd: "Nationalism itself requires the absorption or transformation of justifiable but nonetheless irrational acts of resistance into the self-legitimating form of a political struggle for the state" (Lloyd, 126). The siege of Drogheda, therefore, whatever the intricacies and nuances of historical hermeneutics, enters the canon of Irish nationalism as the zenith and epitome of the essential nature of English colonial intent in Ireland, unmasked in all its brutal and violent manifestations. In *Cromwell,* Drogheda becomes an unspoken justification for nail-bomb attacks by the Provisional IRA in an unspecified contemporary setting (*C,* 135), thus bridging three hundred years of violent history, a series of connections noted by Jonathan Allison:

> *Cromwell* is a powerful poetic study of the problem of violence in Anglo-Irish relations, although it offers little in the way of a vision of how the "patterns of violence" might end. By tracing continuous patterns of revenge from 1641 to the present, Kennelly does adumbrate the continuities between moments of brutal hegemonic domination and brutal resistance, although it is arguable that the poems suggest a predestined propensity to violence which is eternally inescapable.

> But for those who live in Ireland, this is how it often
> feels, and Kennelly's task has been to render that
> emotion of despair, rather than to provide a blueprint
> for a new political dispensation. (Pine, 1994: 88)

Throughout *Cromwell*, therefore, Kennelly attempts to portray Irish history as, in Terry Eagleton's words, a "sprawling limitless web" composed of a "constant interchange and circulation of elements" (Eagleton, 1983: 129) in which no fixed and definitive interpretation of Oliver Cromwell is allowed to emerge unquestioned or unchallenged. The postcolonial model of Irish history as favoured by the new Free State government and expounded by Eamon de Valera relied on a historical perspective of the honourable struggle of the Irish people against the essentially cruel nature of British rule. The complexities of the colonial relationship and the degree of social, cultural and political co-operation and interplay was denied in favour of a polarised version of history that sought out figures like Oliver Cromwell and demonised them to the degree that the latter became symbolic, perhaps ultimately so, of the violence and moral depravity of the British colonial machine. There were influential elements within the Free State that sought to construct a fixed historical interpretation in which the past became a simple paradigm of the oppressor and the oppressed, excluding the possibility of unstable and shifting interpretations of that history and it is precisely in this framework that Kennelly achieves his critical importance. *Cromwell* represents a move towards what Vijay Mishra and Bob Hodge refer to as a "'new' postcolonialism which would take us beyond the oppositional postcolonialism of non-settler colonies that pivots around the moment of independence" (Mishra and Hodge, 1993: 289). The poem points to an interpretation of history that resists absolute meanings and seeks to illuminate the connections inherent in any complex colonial relationship, focusing on the details that simultaneously confirm and deny existing interpretations. Terry Eagleton argues that post-structuralism "strikes a serious blow at certain traditional theories of meaning" (Eagleton, 1983: 129) in much the same way as Kennelly's *Cromwell* strikes a blow at traditional historical interpretations of Ireland's colonial past in general and Oliver Cromwell's role in that past in particular. Kennelly's stated belief in poetry as "connection" (*ATFV*, 12) implies that the attempt to read fixed meanings into both language and history denies a crucial complexity that underpins all historical systems. By the end of *Cromwell*, Buffun is able only to conclude by recognising the multiplicity of selves that compose his imagination and he recognises, crucially, that the past pervades the present in an evolving thread of interpretation that is open-ended, unstable and uncertain.

In the course of the poem, Kennelly clearly attempts to illustrate that the apparently binary oppositions of English and Irish, Catholic and Protestant, Oppressor and Oppressed, Coloniser and Colonised, can be viewed as inextricably linked in the dynamics of a fluid interchange of time, space and individual identity. Indeed, despite his personal suffering and questioning, Buffun offers a way out of the potentially stifling atmosphere of Ireland's colonial and postcolonial identity by loosening the rigidity of ideological stances and it is precisely this type of intellectual liberation that is offered in *Cromwell*. In "Vintage", for example, Buffun reflects:

> I remember thinking, as the blood escaped
> Into the earth, that Oliver did what Oliver did.
> So did the butcher. So do I. So do we all. (*C*, 147)

Despite the apparent simplicity, this is one of the most significant acknowledgements by Buffun that he is moving towards a more pragmatic and less traumatised acceptance of the nature of history and society. Buffun would appear to have transcended the blood that has spilled around him and what emerges is not the reasons for the shedding of the blood but the universality of the act of shedding. Everyone is guilty. Everyone has blood on their hands. This is a critical admission by Buffun and a sign that at least he is struggling to overcome the consequences of the violence and as such it is a crucial and significant point in the poem. Cromwell's assertions that he was merely doing God's work, or that the massacre at Drogheda was designed to avoid further bloodshed, and personal characteristics such as the care and concern he feels for his children and his religious sincerity, are deliberately ignored and excluded from Irish nationalist historiography because each trait could possibly be worked tenaciously through to the point where it threatens to dismantle the oppositions which govern the text as a whole. Add to this the atrocities carried out by Catholics on Protestants in 1641 and the edifice of Oliver Cromwell begins to look a less secure foundational principle upon which to base a nationalist political ideology. Through the interaction of Buffun and Cromwell, the demonisation of the latter becomes increasingly more about Buffun's identity crisis than the reality of Cromwell's activities. It is, after all, Buffun who endures the nightmares and it is he who has to make sense of the past and not Cromwell, paralleling the responsibility placed on postcolonial societies *vis-à-vis* their colonial experience. Buffun even hopes that at the end of his nightmare he will be able to sit outside a pub with Cromwell "sipping infinite pints of cool beer" (*C*, 117), a realisation of his desire to come to terms with and accept the legacy of the past.

The freedom offered in *Cromwell* occurs through an engagement with what Kennelly refers to as the "forbidden figures" (*BS*, 11) of the imagination, be it the Irish peasant stereotype or the ultimate manifestation of English colonial intent. By voicing these figures, Kennelly commits Benedict Anderson's "sacrilege" (Anderson, 1983: 9) through his depiction of the contradictions and hypocrisies at the heart of crucial national cultural icons. The poem undermines and corrodes the hegemonies that seek to paralyse debate over concepts of personal/national identity and as such plays a hugely significant role in the emergence of a critical counter-culture. Consequently, *Cromwell* is unquestioningly one of the most important long poems to be published in Ireland in the twentieth century and it establishes Kennelly at the forefront of a destabilising hermeneutical poetics.

Chapter Four

The Chaos of the Mind: *Medea*

> I am convinced that we have two or three poets in
> France who would be able to translate Homer very well;
> but I am equally convinced that nobody will read them
> unless they soften and embellish almost everything be-
> cause, Madame, you have to write for your own time,
> not for the past. (Voltaire, quoted in Lefevre, 1992: 28)

As early as 1720, Voltaire had arrived at the heart of a linguis-
tic dilemma that echoes through the work of some of the
most influential and popular Irish poets of the twenty-first
century. Such diverse talents as Tom Paulin, Seamus Heaney
and Desmond Egan have turned their attention to classical
Greek drama in an attempt to further examine the complex
nature of Ireland's contemporary postcolonial condition.
Their chosen texts reflect the violence, betrayal and sense of
personal crisis that characterise not only the original Greek
play but the context of its contemporary manifestation. The
most prolific interpreter of these classical texts, however, has
been Brendan Kennelly, whose classical versions include
Medea (1991), *The Trojan Women* (1993) and *Antigone* (1996),
as well as a version of Federico Garcia Lorca's *Blood Wedding*
(1996), further evidence of Kennelly's eclectic output. For the
purposes of this chapter, I will concentrate on his version of
Medea as it most closely parallels many of the themes and

stylistic features of the more prominent poetry and it provides the best example of his reworking of this specific genre.

While his Greek heroines, from Antigone to Medea, rage against their oppressors and exact a terrible revenge on those who cross them, Kennelly's versions are characterised by his ability to bring the texts and the emotions they express into a highly charged contemporary linguistic realm. The violence experienced by women in contemporary Ireland, from the overtly physical to the elision of their personal experiences, drives Kennelly's versions and injects a passion into the texts that resonates with a sharper contemporary social and cultural critique. Kennelly is certainly writing for his own time, delving into and becoming energised by the extreme verbal and physical violence of *Medea*, arguably the most successful of his three plays. The sense of betrayal and the ends to which Medea will go to avenge this overwhelming emotional drive are precisely the familiar territory into which Kennelly has often ventured. The play easily lends itself to his vituperative, highly personal interpretations, yet exactly what specifically Irish dimension emerges is a more complex question and one that needs to be further explored.

There is, of course, a strong personal attraction between Kennelly and his subject. In 1986, he spent the summer in St Patrick's Hospital in Dublin, recovering from a prolonged period of alcoholism. In the hospital, he listened to the stories of women berating their fathers, sons and, most commonly, husbands, men characterised by their unerring ability to let down almost everybody who relied upon them. As recalled by Kennelly, their "unutterable hurt" (*M*, 7) echo Medea's rejection of the "plausible" Jason, a cool and calculating promoter of his own self-interest. The men of these women's stories lie, cheat, break promises, physically assault and drunkenly abuse the women and children in their lives. These women are themselves driven to refuge in alcohol, thereby perpetuating their sense of victimisation. Their revenge finds expression in their anger, and clearly Kennelly drew parallels with these intensely personal stories and the experience of Medea.

While their stories are described by Kennelly as the initial inspiration for his version of Medea, there can be little doubt that his own decision to attempt a resolution of chronic alcoholism provided a focal point for his creative energies. He deliberately mentions this crucial juncture in his life in the introduction to the Bloodaxe version of the play, and there can be little doubt that Medea's anger, which gradually hardens to a cool, moral detachment by the end of the play, reflects Kennelly's own difficulties at the time. Interestingly, in the same introduction, Kennelly recognises in himself the men described by these women, thereby establishing a form of authorial connection with Jason. He recognises the lies, the deceit and the destruction of family life that goes hand-in-hand with any chronic dependency, be it alcohol, social status or economic power, empathising with both Medea and Jason, thereby cleverly blurring the distinction between the perception of who is victim and who is victimiser. Few characters emerge from Kennelly's play with any integrity, the heroine least of all. Medea's final exchange with Jason highlights the fact that his suffering is paramount and Medea's justifications for her actions appear increasingly petty and spiteful. Perhaps for Kennelly this is the only resolution possible: that no life is free from its torment and no action can be wrought without consequences.

Kennelly's stated belief that a marriage "can be a kind of violent, exclusive intimacy" (Kennelly, 1994: 14) certainly rings true in his version of the play and the protagonists play out an all-too-familiar tragedy. Medea tells the audience that Jason was "my sun, my moon and my stars, my sacred rivers and holy mountains" (M, 24), only to be revealed, after he has acquired what he needs, as a "poisonous snake". Marriage proves to be the "revelation", a state of freefall as Jason exhibits "a sudden loss of interest in her body", leading to Medea's social exclusion. Often in the play Medea speaks for women in general, directly appealing to the women in the audience to listen and to respond with their "silence", what Medea refers to as "the most powerful weapon of all", and this motif of silence features regularly in Kennelly's work and in various texts in Irish literature in general. In John B. Keane's *The Field*, for example, the visiting bishop berates mass-goers over their communal silence regarding the murder of an outsider who sought to buy a valuable local field that was the *de facto* possession of the Bull McCabe. He states:

> The church bell will be silent: the mass bell will not be heard; the voice of the confessional will be stilled and in your last moment will be the most dreadful silence of all, for you will go to face your Maker without the last sacrament on your lips . . . and all because of your silence now. (Keane, 1990: 150)

Given Keane and Kennelly's north Kerry heritage, it would appear that this concept of a self-protective silence shared by members of a community is a feature of Medea that would have particular resonance within Kennelly's own local community and might again prove to be a source of attraction with the play.

There are, of course, difficult questions that have to be faced in any assessment of a "version" of another author's work. Kennelly must follow some of the narrative structure of the play, and is morally unable to escape entirely the Aristotelian constriction of the plot. His Medea will be betrayed by Jason and infamously commit filicide as Euripides' Medea has done, and herein lie both the strengths and weakness of this type of drama. His only real freedom within the text is, arguably, the most powerful freedom of all, namely the reconstruction of the words of the characters in an attempt to contemporise the very morality that places these plays in the literary canon in the first place. Kennelly remains relatively faithful to the roles of the nurse and the chorus, both of whom retain their roles of moral interpreters of the action. The complex role of Medea as both feminist icon and heartless killer (interpretations which ironically hinge upon each other) cannot be altered by Kennelly to the degree that her actions are changed. Her psyche, however, is open territory and his role in constructing a world vision in which her actions can begin to be understood is crucial. His Medea is a complicated and contradictory character, her confused morality exemplified by the murder of the children.

In the intervening twenty-four centuries between Euripides and Kennelly, however, the social, political, sexual and cultural roles of women have radically altered and therefore contemporary interpreters of Medea have to present the play in the light of an audience that is less likely to be impressed by the portrayal of an independent woman than their ancient Greek counterparts. This, however, is not to argue that the cultural situation is unrecognisable; Kennelly has clearly indicated, through his dialogue and plot, that certain human traits, invariably negative ones, have altered only in terms of the context rather than the content. It is these traits (jealousy, revenge, violence) that give the drama its edge and yet curiously it is the plot that restricts real character development. For example, in one of the blurbs on the back of the Bloodaxe edition, Oliver Taplin writing for the *Times Literary Supplement* rightly acknowledges the "great verbal virtuosity" of Kennelly's play but curiously also celebrates its "unpredictable" nature. How unpredictable can a version of Euripides' play be when it largely follows the plot outline and development of the source text? Surely most audiences would be familiar with the original plot and therefore have certain expectations. Kennelly, however, appears to concentrate on making the play relevant to a contemporary audience rather than attempting to make the audience aware of the Greek conventions that the play explores.

This crucial distinction is clearly visible in the recognisable Kennellian dialogic interchange between the characters. His

Medea is initially humanly unhappy, rightly enraged with her husband, a man she gave up everything for, yet she cascades into an anger that appears superhuman, prepared to subvert all moral conventions in an attempt to satisfy her revenge. Her anger is portrayed, not only as a righteous personal anger against the man who wronged her, but as a larger complaint and note of resistance against various forms of institutionalised violence meted out to women. Her anger spills out into a diatribe against the falsity of Athenian city life where "style" is more highly regarded than "honour"(*M*, 41). The city is a place where women are subject to the "lawful barbarisms" of men who are portrayed as the "horny despots of our bodies" (*M*, 25). These "blind, ambitious, power-hungry cretins" (*M*, 42) clog the streets in their headlong rush for material success, oblivious to the emotional carnage they leave behind them. By the end of the play, Medea has clearly illustrated to Jason, in the most violent manner imaginable, that the very social and political structures he wishes to control cannot protect him from pure human vengeance. Indeed, the impotence of institutions when faced with the wrath of an aggrieved individual, or individuals, is an issue that has crucial contemporary relevance.

When Fintan O'Toole wrote in 1992, apropos the exposure of the love-child of Bishop Eamon Casey, that one of the options facing the Irish hierarchy was that of "the bishop as man, fallen, fallible, having no authority but the one that matters: the authority of experience" (O'Toole, 1994: 137), he could well be describing Jason, a man, as described by Medea, who "gambled and lost" (*M*, 74). She labels him a "poor, sad, pointless man" (*M*, 74), stripped of the veneer of power and authority that he so valued. Indeed, O'Toole's description of Casey's affair with Annie Murphy reads remarkably like the story of *Medea* itself:

> He dazzles her with his power, his confidence, his command of the world. They fall in love and begin a

sexual relationship. He promises her nothing, but he doesn't need to, for hurt and abused as she is, she is more than capable of making him into a promise to herself. She gives him pleasure, excitement and adoration. He gives her the first two but probably not the third. She thinks of the future, he thinks of the present, floating on the delusion that he can have the best of all worlds. He makes her pregnant. The baby forces choices on her, choices which, because he is a man and a powerful one, he doesn't believe he has to make. He behaves badly, hypocritically, politically. It ends in tears: first hers, then, after many years, his. (O'Toole, 1994: 139)

What one associates most with Euripides' Medea, and indeed provides a source of morbid fascination, is the fact that she murders her two children in an act of ultimate revenge on Jason, and her reasoning of this peculiarly unnatural act is one of the key narratives driving Kennelly's version. The act of filicide appears to question one of our most basic human moral precepts, that of the protection and nurturing of children. Of course, it can easily be viewed as a tired misogynistic portrayal of the killer woman, so obsessed with the man in her life that she is prepared to kill her children to avenge his betrayal. Equally, her actions can be viewed as the ultimate act of feminist liberation, freedom from the perceived emotional bondage of motherhood. Kennelly's Medea appears so consumed with her rage that the filicide appears less brutal than it otherwise might, the children almost necessary victims in the crossfire between husband and wife. Her children were created with Jason, therefore they are a constant reminder to her of his eternal proximity and are thus doomed. Despite the best efforts of the nurse, Medea damns both the children and their father in the same breath, frighteningly reminiscent of suicidal parents who decide that their children must die with them. In Ireland, the average murder rate of children in the period 1998–2000 was six; the taking of children by a suicidal parent is an occurrence that brings the often bizarre nature of parental love into sharp relief. In certain circumstances, the suicidal parent regards it as the ultimate expression of love, and Kennelly's desire to explore such an apparently unnatural and complex manifestation of human behaviour is entirely consistent with the rest of his work.

In Philip Vellacott's translation for Penguin Classics, Medea, showing her cool but perverse logic, declares that "I'll not leave sons of mine to be the victims of my enemies' rage" (Vellacott, 1963: 50). Kennelly, on the other hand, has Medea acknowledging that "passion strangles my love" (*M*, 66), a position that certainly places a different emphasis on the reasons for the perceived necessity of the children's death. Medea does not kill herself as this would appear as a Jasonic triumph and, indeed, she only embarks on her murderous revenge when an escape route to Athens has been prearranged. However, she is well aware of the effect the death of the children will have on Jason. Equally, a fundamental question of love arises in the case of filicide: to what extent are parents who commit suicide protecting their children by taking them with them? At the moment of her children's deaths, Medea exhibits that combination of fierce passion and steely will that characterises her movement through the play. The love she forlornly seeks from Jason swamps whatever maternal feelings she might have and the children end their life exactly as they began it; directly as a consequence of the tumultuous union of husband and wife. However, whether it can be regarded as Medea's ultimate triumph is a hugely debatable question. While she certainly inflicts her desired revenge on Jason, what is she left with as she escapes to Athens on her fiery chariot? According to the Chorus (in the Penguin Classics text) "The unexpected God makes possible" (Vellacott, 1963: 61), and in the final analysis, perhaps this is all we know and all we need to know.

The Chaos of the Mind: Medea

The freedom offered by the "version" moniker allows Kennelly the opportunity to explore the familiar territory of the marginalised, the socially excluded and those whose behaviour sets them apart from the norms of social discourse. It is precisely in this contentious area of the "unvoiced" that elements of contemporary postcolonial theory shed fascinating light on Kennelly's body of work and on new interpretations of those perceived to be at both the centre and margins of cultural, political and sexual discourses. Homi K. Bhabha asserts that it is in "those moments or processes that are produced in the articulation of cultural differences" (Bhabha, 1994: 1–2), such as those between Jason and Medea, the Greek and the outsider, that crucial composite elements in cultural identities begin to emerge. Jason's self-righteousness and, particularly in Kennelly's text, his bumptious self-importance wither when juxtaposed directly with the passion of Medea. He represents a civilised, orderly existence in which marriage has a clear social and economic function. Medea, as a non-Greek, could never be recognised as his wife and she represents the passionate, instinctual barbarian, and it is precisely in the confrontation between Greek and barbarian that Greek society is defined. Jason's eventual tragedy results from his inability to reconcile these opposites, and his incredulous response to Medea's murder of the children highlights his personal removal from the emotional aspects of his psyche.

Throughout his poetry, Kennelly has flirted with opposites, his poetic instincts heightened by characters that have to deal with a rational and safe life that is haunted by madness and an unquenched recklessness. Jason and Medea are two clear voices that inhabit every individual, personifying the shifting entity that is selfhood. Kennelly has said that self "is always open to change and development, what the moral self might call betrayal" (quoted in Pine, 1994: 171), and perhaps it is this very lack of openness that seals Jason's fate, and indeed renders Medea unable to cope with the changes in her marital

circumstances. His *Medea* presents a world vision of compet-
ing ideologies and the adherence of both Jason and Medea to
their respective beliefs results in the ultimate destruction of
their relationship and the deaths of four innocent people.

It is only through the moderating influence of the Chorus at
the beginning of Part Two that Kennelly overtly describes the
potential middle ground between the politically inspired aspira-
tions of Jason and the raw, emotional openness of Medea. The
sensitive and sensible perspective of the Chorus provides the
play with a much-needed objective correlative but in many ways
this only serves to highlight the intensity of Medea's emotions.
The Chorus declares that "to live within limits is to honour the
infinite, mysterious potential of excess", a fascinating insight
given Kennelly's personal battle with alcohol at the time, a
thought that resonates with Kavanagh's brilliantly simple maxim
that "through a chink too wide comes in no wonder"
(Kavanagh, 1996: 146). Kennelly's play is arguably less con-
cerned with grand national narratives and codes of behaviour
than with, as Kathleen McCracken notes, "the feminist impera-
tives and, by extension, the broad humanist ramifications" (Pine,
1994: 121) that emerge from the narrative. However, it would
not do full justice to Kennelly's version to ignore the larger
ramifications of national identity that he had so brilliantly eluci-
dated eight years previously in *Cromwell*.

Kennelly's text, however, is more complex than a mere
re-reading of a classic text in a contemporary light. If one ac-
cepts Kennelly's traditionally subversive poetic role, then
Medea's actions cannot be merely explained away as the justi-
fiable actions of a woman scorned. What mention or regard
is taken of Jason's undoubted suffering at the loss of his chil-
dren? Is the experience of men to again be written out of the
text as a mere exemplar of their pathological and unques-
tioned unworthiness? Indeed, it is the two children, signifi-
cantly both male, who pay the ultimate price for their
mother's scorn, begging the question as to the real nature of

a sense of victimisation in the text. Despite all her acknowl-
edged bitterness, Medea flees at the end of the play; Jason is
left in mourning, while their children lie dead. Who else can
be regarded as the true victims, other than the children, or is
the sentence of living with a loved one's murder a greater
punishment, as Medea suggests? Although Medea's rage and
sense of betrayal inevitably form the thematic basis of the
majority of criticism of the play, Jason and the other men ap-
pear as social-climbing, sexually obsessed stooges, mono-
dimensional characters who pale into insignificance when jux-
taposed with the passionate, determined Medea. Aegeus, for
example, is more than happy to overlook Medea's murderous
actions on the promise that she will provide him with chil-
dren, an example of Medea's inability to learn from her past
experiences, a repetition of her husband's behaviour that
Medea appears content enough to ignore.

Interestingly, Kennelly's Greek trilogy feature women as
their protagonists, and this is again a consistent feature of
Kennelly's work as many of his poems attempt to "voice"
women, a precarious undertaking for a male poet but one
which Kennelly manages through, according to Kathleen
McCracken, "the displacement of the self with what is the
other" (Pine, 1994: 117), an instantly recognisable Kennellian
hermeneutic. Including *A Girl* (1981) and his translation of
Mary (1987), Kennelly has consistently sought to adopt,
amongst a phalanx of others, a female perspective, which he
describes in the introduction to *The Trojan Women* as a
"complex reality of . . . mesmeric intensities (*TW*, 5) and
Medea provides him with a suitably dramatic vehicle to con-
tinue this vicarious exploration.

Ironically, the majority of the modern Irish versions of
classical Greek drama have been written by men, yet the ex-
perience of women appears paramount. Are poets still afraid
to write about the suffering of men because they may appear
to simultaneously elide the experience of women? Is the fear

also apparent that in writing about the male characters the poets might appear to tread on the toes of feminist interpretations of the tragedies? Interestingly, the poetic sensitivities are heightened when describing the emotions of the female other but appear less concerned with the social and cultural pressures that formed the likes of Jason in the first place. Kennelly overtly describes his play as concerned with the "rage" of women "mainly against men, Irishmen like myself" (M, 7) and the clear implication in the text is of Medea being driven to her wits' end by the pathological wanderings of her husband. Indeed, Euripides' play begins at the point of Jason's betrayal of Medea, rather than with the various acts of murderous collusion that characterised their early relationship, including Medea's betrayal of her father Aeetes and the brutal murder of her own brother, Apsyrtus. Is Euripides also refusing to see the entire picture for fear that the creation of his feminist icon might appear more complicated than his play allows? Would the audience's Medean empathy be tarnished by the dramatic scene of Medea chopping up the body of her brother and scattering it from the back of her fleeing boat? Equally, imagine the torment of Creon and Glauce as Medea's poisoned crown burns the flesh from their bodies?

A critique of the portrayal of men in *Medea* is not a covert Freudian admission of fear or admonishment of Jason's betrayal but rather a filling in of a picture that, occasionally, appears very lopsided. An exception to this portrayal certainly occurs at the end of the play when Jason's obvious and genuine grief for the death of his sons appears to overwhelm him. It is only at this point that he appears to express genuine human emotion rather than the politically driven social-climbing shibboleths of the previous scenes. However, Kennelly leaves his readers no doubt about the real victor in all of this emotional mess by concluding his version with this controversial line:

Is Medea's crime also Medea's glory? (M, 75)

The rhetorical nature of this question implicitly suggests that Kennelly's sympathies lie squarely with Medea and that, indeed, the murder of her children has been a literal and symbolic act of liberation. Certainly Kennelly's perception of the liberation of Medea from the traditional shackles of child-rearing and child love is a challenging and stimulating perspective and this final line certainly places Kennelly's version at odds with the standard conclusion of other versions and translations of the play. Is Medea's "glory" the fact that, unlike Thomas Hardy's tragic heroine Tess of the d'Urbervilles, she ultimately gets away with her murderous revenge? Perhaps it is in this outcome that Kennelly finds the attraction of the play. In drama, as in other forms of literature, an all-pervading naturalist morality suggests that all wrongdoers will ultimately pay for their crime, yet Medea triumphantly leaves the broken Jason on her chariot and lives out an eventful life in Athens. Alongside Electra, she succeeds in her revenge, emerging from the play like a pre-modern Terminator, leaving behind her the obligatory body-count of discarded mortals who cross her ill-starred path.

Medea's description of Jason as a "plausible man", skilled in the art of verbal deception, suggests a theme that has concerned Kennelly from his earliest poetic works. In the last poem of *The Boats Are Home*, "Six of One", for example, he exposes the "barbarian", a man secure in his own self-importance and unafraid to fill the perceived vacuum in the minds of those he meets. Remaining blissfully unaware of his own inadequacies, "he makes articulate the pitifully dumb" (*TBAH*, 52), robbing language from the mouths of those he deems as unworthy or incapable of self-expression. Again in *The Visitor*, the ubiquitous house guest struts into a house and, through his own delusions of self-importance and an inability to recognise the needs of those around him, proceeds to "rob" the children "of every word they had" by filling their spaces with his stories (*TBAH*, 29). In Kennelly's poetry, this form of linguistic violence is perpetrated by teachers against pupils, priests against congregation, parent against child, husband against wife and almost anybody who is placed in a position of trust by another. "Love and you will be betrayed" is a constant theme throughout his work and the closer the relationship the deeper the sense of betrayal. The emotional investment in the visitor by the children is cruelly discarded by his vain and over-inflated sense of self-importance and the poem ends with the tragic silence of the woman and her children, victims of the super-ego that sweeps all before it.

Kennelly is a skilled demythologiser of language, always prepared to go beyond the semantic surface into the deeper realms of power, control and violence that lie at the heart of linguistic systems. The violence meted out in polite words is the most common violence of all. Medea castigates Jason, accusing him of a "plausibility" that "smothers the soul with oily words", preferring "a passionately meant insult" which, as a consequence of its honesty, acts as "a kind of compliment" (*M*, 40). However, this appearance of respectability is unmasked by "one burning word of honesty", the plausible man uncovered in all his duplicity. In much the same way as Roland Barthes lamented the inevitable fate of the farmer Dominici, faced with the labyrinthine linguistic constructions of the legal world, so Kennelly's Jason remains neutered by his passionless language, his Greek manners and upbringing withering in the face of his wife's untamed and ferocious passion.

Barthes's brilliant study of Gaston Dominici's 1952 trial for murder concludes that the accused faced the ultimate terror, that of "being judged by a power which wants to hear only the language it lends us" (Barthes, 1997: 42). Jason undoubtedly suffers that fate at the pens of not only Kennelly but other translators of *Medea*. He is rendered almost mute, unable to move beyond platitudinous defences of his position, defences that are increasingly undermined by Medea's verbal onslaught. Barthes posits the view that "to rob a man of his language in

the very name of language is the first step in all legal murders"
(Barthes, 1997: 46) and, interestingly, it is Jason, and perhaps
more significantly the two boys, who are robbed of their lan-
guage by Medea. Euripides failed to include the boys' stories in
his play, and by extension Jason's story remains partially told,
the detail and emphasis provided by Medea. Equally, the mur-
der of the children has traditionally been seen as part of an
overall dramatic convention. John Ferguson has written, "The
death of the children is transfigured by being seen as part of
timeless sorrow. To understand this is to understand the soul
of Greek tragedy; to fail to understand this is to leave empty
formalism and dead convention" (Ferguson, 1972: 263). Now
to use the term "death" in relation to two children who are
consciously and deliberately led to their murder can quite rea-
sonably be assumed in itself to lean towards empty formalism
and thus a different and challenging perspective on the play can
begin to emerge. The strength of Kennelly's *Medea*, therefore,
lies precisely in the text's ability to arouse a variety of re-
sponses that depend almost entirely upon the reader's social,
cultural and political stance, a classic example of Barthes's no-
tion that the reader is "simply someone who holds together in
a single field all the traces by which the written text is consti-
tuted" (quoted in Lodge, 1988: 171).

Needless to say, it would also be a travesty to view Ken-
nelly's Jason as some kind of postmodern masculinist icon.
His prime motivation in wooing Glauce reflects his desire to
move beyond what he perceives to be his lowly station in life.
He tells Medea that "it was not for the sake of a woman that
I enter marriage", arguing that he wanted "royalty to spread
through my family", endeavouring "to distance myself from
poverty and shame" (*M*, 41). His justification resonates with
postcolonial Ireland's attempt to distance itself from the pov-
erty of its colonial past, embracing wholeheartedly a neo-
colonial economics that brings with it the consequent dilution
of a distinctive cultural identity. He cannot, or at best will

not, understand Medea's reaction to his stated desire to im-
prove the social position of his children and, by extension,
Medea herself. His shallowness is exposed and ultimately
proves to be his undoing.

Medea, equally, is a complex mixture of contradictions, an
attractive proposition for a poet like Kennelly. Despite the
fact that her brother has been murdered in her inevitably vain
search for personal happiness, she proceeds to claim that "I
want the happiness that comes from my husband and my
children" (M, 41), a claim that appears hollow in the light of
her subsequent murder of the very children she mentions as
central to her idea of happiness. In many ways, these
contradictions lie at the heart of Medea's attraction. She
eludes definition or categorisation, her words and actions
coinciding and diverging with no apparent consistency, driven
solely by her vengeful desires. She admits that her one great
error was the betrayal of her father, yet she proceeds to kill
her two children in an attempt to gain revenge on Jason.

If it is accepted that one of the central features of contem-
porary versions is the translation of cultures as well as words,
then surely the subversive nature of Euripides' original work
has to be viewed in the context of intervening social and cul-
tural movements and theories. Given that Euripides' Athens
"was a place in which Pericles proclaimed that the greatest
glory of woman is not to be spoken of by men for good or
bad" (Ferguson, 1972: 239), then certainly a play in which a
woman is allowed not only to express her emotions but to
carry out her revenge to such devastating effect has to be seen
as wonderfully challenging of the cultural orthodoxy of its time.
Equally, Kennelly's experience of the battered, abused and
marginalised women he came across in St Patrick's Hospital in
the summer of 1986 finds a powerful expression in the play.
His Medea is angry to the point of not caring about the long-
term personal consequences of her anger, hinting at a rejection
of traditional stoical acceptance of male abuse. Writing at a

critical juncture in his own life, Kennelly understands Medea's anger, a vortex of self-loathing that manifests itself in the attempt to destroy all those who come close to her, culminating in the elimination of the only people who are directly of her own flesh. Perhaps she has to kill her children to stand any chance of recovering what little sanity has been afforded her. Attempting to break the grip of alcohol, Kennelly empathises with a character that is driven to pathological unhappiness, almost relishing the darkness and chaos that typifies her existence. Alcoholism is a lonely pursuit, an existence dogged by a paranoia that distrusts all those who seek to help. The concept of a recovery only being possible when the alcoholic realises their own predicament echoes Medea's repeated rejection of the advice of the Chorus, the teacher and the nurse. The one person who empathises with Medea is Medea, as secure as her chaotic mind will allow in her mono-focal drive to avenge.

However, Kennelly's Medea, and for that matter other Irish versions of Greek tragedy, have emerged on the coat-tails of Marxist, feminist, psychoanalytic and postcolonial critical theories and the impact of these ideas on the readers and writers of contemporary versions cannot be underestimated. For example, the elision of the psyche of Jason and the children from the story presents the contemporary reader with grave difficulties. Postcolonial theory in general, and subaltern studies in particular, seeks out the stories of those whose experiences have formed a central plank of the colonial or postcolonial exercise but who have been excluded from cultural discourses because their articulation would upset traditional and accepted perceptions of history, culture and society. Indeed, the elision of Jason's story in the text would place him in the interesting position of subalternity, a central theoretical element in postcolonial theory in which the stories and histories of the excluded achieve articulation. Although Jason would not be traditionally considered subaltern, given his high social position, economic wealth and royal connections, his story in the play is merely hinted at, with the vast majority of emotional insight and expression reserved for Medea. Jason's role is to complete the binary of betrayer/betrayed, but his reasoning is largely dismissed, while the chorus concludes that Medea's filicide is understandable given her treatment. Clearly, his story exists in the same realm as the mute children of "The Visitor", destined to be articulated and contextualised by another.

Medea's anger flows freely, her complex character invigorated by an outpouring of revenge virtually unparalleled in classical or contemporary literature. Her story is told. Jason, despite his infidelity, is the pillar of Greek manners and his story is not told, at least not to the same degree as Medea's. Kennelly's Jason chastises Medea with "my instinctive wisdom", "the sanity and rightness of my choice" and refers to the "noble service" he has rendered his wife and sons. His myopia is confounded when he states, to almost comic effect, that "women should not exist". His argument is so fundamentally flawed as to appear mock-tragic and certainly we find out little about his true motivations other than the trite stereotypical male concerns for a better material life for him and his children. As a straight man, he works very well. Medea's response allows Jason no room for manoeuvre in that she decries "the plausible traitor" as "the worst scoundrel", strangling Jason's defence at birth and cleverly using her anger to portray him as uncaring and mono-dimensional.

Kennelly has long been attracted to such powerful figures primarily because they avoid the ontological questioning that is such a feature of Kennelly's work. He acknowledges as much in the introduction to *A Time for Voices*:

> Powerful figures such as The Visitor and Cromwell attract me because they act as if they were intensely one in themselves, dramatically and passionately present to themselves and to others, sure of their own voices, capable of uniting fragmented people about them. (*ATFV*, 13)

In his introduction to the text, Kennelly makes no reference to a translated text of *Medea* upon which his version is based, contenting himself by referring to "the Medea that I tried to imagine" (*M*, 8) as his guiding principle. This arguably gives Kennelly greater freedom over his material in that while remaining faithful to the traditionally accepted outline and development of the plot, he ascribes to himself the ultimate freedom of linguistic interpretation. The shaping of dialogic interchange and the manipulation of words empowers Kennelly's Medea to escape the constraints of accepted versions of the original text. For example, in Philip Vellacott's translation for Penguin Classics (1963: 31), Medea attacks Jason on her first encounter with him since his betrayal of her:

> You filthy coward! — if I knew any worse name
> For such unmanliness I'd use it — so, you've come.

For a woman skilled in magic and prepared to go to any lengths to avenge her battered pride, it seems odd that she cannot come up with any words worse than "you filthy coward!". In Kennelly's version, however, his traditional penchant for the venomous *mot just* comes to the fore as Medea vents her spleen on her traitorous husband:

> Stink of the grave, rot of a corpse's flesh,
> slime of this putrid world,
> unburied carcass of a dog in the street,
> the black-and-yellow greeny spit of a drunk at midnight —
> these are my words for you. (*M*, 36)

Kennelly's version of the anger of this encounter presents a very different Medea to the somewhat restrained Vellacott version. In the latter version, her anger is very Anglo-Saxon, restrained, controlled and yet hinting at a fierce retribution to follow. The Irish Medea, however, has no such hindrances. Indeed, the impression is given that Medea could have carried on in this vituperative Falstaffian vein for quite some time, flaunting her insults as her anger increased. The expression of anger is as important to Kennelly's Medea as the practical actions she carries out in the venting of that anger. Consequently, through this manipulation of the dialogue, Kennelly gives a very different portrait of Medea, a woman whose ability to carry out acts of the deadliest ferocity is matched by her desire to express her anger in the clearest possible terms. Therefore, the question arises as to which Medea is most to be feared: the volcanic Medea who openly rants about her hatred for Jason or the more restrained, threatening Medea whose silences are as threatening as her words, if not more so? It is precisely in these areas of contestation that the vitality and imagination of the interpreter comes to the fore.

For Kennelly, this voicing of bilious anger is a recurring poetic motif and it comes as no surprise that his Medea should be so adept at expressing her anger in such terms. In an essay dealing directly with the link between poetry and violence, Kennelly asks a seminal question: "what do we do with the violence of our emotions?" (Kennelly, 1994: 28) and in so many of his poems, his characters content themselves with the cathartic power of expression, imploding in violent words and images that in many ways dilute the need for direct reparative action. Medea, therefore, might appear as an unusual choice for Kennelly in that her anger is manifested in the utmost physical violence as well as vituperative rhetoric, and it is in this final act of filicide that the central dilemma over Medea lies. Kennelly ends his version with a highly provocative rhetorical question : "Is Medea's crime also Medea's glory?". His play ends with a question as to the nature of Medea's existence, a question which she herself appears to answer in her final contact with Jason:

> There's nothing of you left in me.
> How much of me is left in you? (*M*, 74)

Chapter Five

Following the Judasvoice

You know I love the element of surprise.
In the garden I was playing the tart
I kissed your lips and broke your heart
You . . . you were acting like it was
the end of the world.
                              — U2, "Until the End of the World"

There can be little doubt that Brendan Kennelly's second epic sequence, *The Book of Judas*, first published by Bloodaxe Books in 1991, amplifies and develops many of the ideological themes and stylistic constructions explored in *Cromwell*. The most obvious development pivots on the centralising of the figure of Judas Iscariot, an internationally recognisable icon of betrayal whose popular treatment parallels the specifically Irish demonisation of Oliver Cromwell. In virtually all areas of the Western world, the name of Judas carries connotations of the deepest and most hurtful betrayal, a figure who was chosen to share in the most intense of relationships but who apparently chose to sell that commitment for a handful of silver. It is in this particular portrait of betrayal that Kennelly finds a vibrant social and political critique and it is a theme that is apparent from his earliest work. In "The Whistler", first published in *Green Townlands*, his 1963 co-production with Rudi Holzapfel,

Kennelly describes the effect of the "wild notes" of a ubiqui-
tous village whistler as the "soft swell of this illusion". This
initial musical experience ultimately allures the "fascinated
heart and ear" and, once it has departed, leaves a "silence that
voids the heart" (*GT*, 6). This is an early warning against the
inevitable and almost irresistible emotional over-investment
that characterises many forms of betrayal and it sets the tone
for Kennelly's continued resistance to the world of polite in-
quiry and linguistic obfuscation. Indeed, in the final poem of
Cromwell, entitled "A Soft Amen", Kennelly hints that his ex-
ploration of his polyvocal psyche has a long way to go:

> . . . all the others striding through me,
> prisoners on parole from history,
> Striving to come alive as I think I am,
> Finding their food in me . . . (*C*, 160)

This concept of a burgeoning and troubled self-expression
also points to another central theme in *The Book of Judas*,
namely the questioning of the ability of poetry to accurately
reflect the intended wishes of the poet and its tendency to
betray the very voice that gives it expression. This debate
over the efficacy of poetry permeates the collection and it
mirrors Judas's often-expressed anxiety over the veracity and
inherent untrustworthiness of his words, memories and ideas.
Indeed, in many of his prose writings, Kennelly has mulled
over the liminal relationship between linguistic constructions
and poetic integrity, arguing that language's fundamental in-
ability to capture the essence of what it is exploring under-
mines whatever claims to authenticity poetry can have.

If Seamus Heaney can famously describe his poetic mis-
sion as "digging" (Heaney, 1966: 13–14), then Kennelly's Judas
could be accused of bobbing along upon the backwash cre-
ated by the "relentless, pitiless, anecdotalism of Irish life" (*J*,
11), sure only that he is a cipher of often vicious vicarious
expression. The implied confidence that Heaney enjoys with

his "snug" pen (Heaney: 1966: 13–14) contrasts sharply with Judas's rhetorical question in the very first poem of the collection entitled "Lips", in which he mulls over how often he had been betrayed by his words:

> They slave for me, ask nothing in return.
> The harder they work the more I wonder
> If I believe them. (*J*, 15)

This uncertainty is one of the collection's greatest strengths. As with *Cromwell*, and indeed in Kennelly's third epic collection *Poetry My Arse* (1995), the reader, complicit in this linguistic binary, has to work at identifying not only the voice that is being articulated at any given time but also the degree of irony, satire and sincerity inherent in its expression. This narrative and explicatory dislocation powers whatever narrative *The Book of Judas* can claim to have and it parallels the preface's stated intention to utilise "the uncertainties of altruistic exploration" (*J*, 9). Indeed, Kennelly's three great interrogative epics have had a long gestation. In 1973, the same year he was appointed Professor of Modern Literature in Trinity College, Dublin, *The Voices* was published and in this collection he explicitly attempts to give "a voice to the unthinkable" (Pine, 1990: 22) and it is a collection which he states "was the beginning of it". In the poem "Heart", for example, the poet is "a dumb stump" (*TV*, 25) who has nothing to say until visited, often unwillingly, by aggressive muses who ironically rely upon a voice they clearly do not respect for their expression. It is as if Kennelly imagines the poet to be engaged in a form of automatic writing, desperately seeking "a clear voice" in a tumult of accreting and competing words, images and memories. In this poem, he appears unable and unwilling to stop the vital expression of these various personae, internal voices that he was later to describe in the final poem of *Cromwell* as "prisoners on parole from history" (*C*, 160).

The poem has strong parallels with Ted Hughes's well-known exposition of his poetic oeuvre, "The Thought Fox", in which Hughes reflects that "something else is alive" (Keegan, 2000: 976) outside of his poetic control, eventually penetrating "the dark hole of the head" in order to find its place of expression. While Hughes's poem eventually appears around "midnight", Kennelly's recalcitrant muse is "keeping him from sleep", disturbing his daylight hours with phantasmagoria requiring frantic and immediate explication. In Kennelly's image, this poetic expression is a violent process, the voices parasitically gnawing away at the sensibility of the poet. *The Voices* concludes with a poem entitled "Word" in which Kennelly gives a clear expression to the *force majeure* that would drive his later epic sequences:

I
Serve
Your most inarticulate cry

From depths you often ignore,
The darkest reason there is
For your brightest endeavour. (*TV*, 30)

This interesting juxtaposition mirrors Kennelly's later and controversial conclusion to *Medea* when he asks the question "Is Medea's crime also Medea's glory?" (*M*, 75), suggestive of the continual drive in Kennelly's work for connections between apparently oppositional forces and individuals. Indeed, throughout *The Book of Judas*, it is clear that Judas's treachery is an integral part of the reason why certain sections of humanity can claim "Christ for an eternal friend" (*GSTS*, 46), a line that first appeared as early as Kennelly's 1967 collection, *Good Souls to Survive*. In the preface to his 1969 *Selected Poems* Kennelly notes that "poetry returns again and again to the same themes", highlighting the "few things" that have concerned him as poet up to that point, principally "the attempt to understand the nature of good and evil" and "the relation-ship of forces such as cruelty and corruption to the human passion and need for survival" (*SP*, 1969, *xii*). Kennelly's poetic development hinges on his continued use of a central narrative voice controlling the expression of competing manifestations of concrete historical figures and a complex interaction be-tween personal and national histories. This poetic protagonist, whose latest manifestation is the first-century AD Roman writer Martial, allows Kennelly a degree of hermeneutical and chronological flexibility, providing his epic collections with a historical narrative that is both familiar to his audience and flexible enough to allow a strong degree of contemporary cul-tural critique. However, this very familiarity allows Kennelly to subvert traditional readings by also articulating the borders of the discourse, casting as wide a net as possible in the search for marginalised voices who speak back to the centre. Ironi-cally, by choosing to centre his poems on recognisable histori-cal figures, Kennelly allows both the centre and the margins to engage in a mutually enlightening exorcism of long-held preju-dices and half-believed mythologies. Consequently, James Joyce can credibly and wittingly have dinner with the Holy Family while Christy Hannitty can attend a conference on cas-tration in Hackballscross, the absurdity of the situations merely highlighting the inherent instability of what passes for contemporary reality.

This constant flux echoes Declan Kiberd's assertion that "identity is seldom straightforward and given, more often a matter of negotiation and exchange" (Kiberd, 1995: 1). Judas's engagement with a variety of key figures in the formation of a popularly held model of Irish identity sheds crucial light on the context in which this identity was fashioned and his bi-zarre exchanges point to a more complex national genesis than that allowed in the popular imagination. This in turn places *The Book of Judas* at the forefront of articulating what Colin Graham refers to as a "continual futurity which can never facilitate full definition" (Graham, 1994: 76) in that the collection's refusal to be bound by spatial restrictions allows Judas unlimited access to not only originary moments in the development of Christianity but also to dialogue with, amongst others, Marilyn Monroe, Adolf Hitler, James Joyce and Brendan Behan. These iconic cultural, political and literary figures expose the charade of the recreation and reinvention of the public and the private in the desperate drive for an authenticity around which models of identity can be constructed. Judas travels easily between Calvary and the inner city of Dublin, their differences evaporating in the commonality of human experience. Both epochs speak to each other, held together by the voice of Judas, which nervously undermines this unity by acknowledging that "both words and silences betray" (*J*, 341).

Kennelly sustains his exploration of the myriad manifestations of betrayal over 584 poems, the disjointed chronology being unwittingly held together by the isolated, irredeemable figure of Judas, an outsider who embraces and absorbs both the forces that exclude and the consequences of that exclusion. He emerges from Kennelly's text as a complex exemplar of the duplicitous nature of social and cultural moral imperatives that seek reductionist interpretations of what are essentially elusive human characteristics. Indeed, the narrator of the poems is more closely allied to what Kennelly identifies in the introduction as the "Judasvoice" (*J*, 11), an often miasmatic articulator of vituperative anger, misogyny, greed, tenderness and denial. As well as his varied contemporary manifestations, Judas also appears in his historical guise, albeit pursued by, amongst others, film crews, journalists and talk-show hosts, and it is in the poems in which Jesus and Judas engage in an often surreal dialogue that the collection achieves its sharpest focus and historical critique.

Iconic historical moments are cleverly contemporised by the abrupt appearance of recognisable social stereotypes, characters whose narrative function is to bring the historical into sharp contemporary relief. The absurdity of the moment, both the historical and the contemporary, is highlighted by their strange parallel expression, the past and the present finding mutually informing moments of both intense illumination and simultaneous farce. One such moment arrives as Jesus is stretched on the cross waiting to be nailed, a defining originary moment in Christianity. However, no one can be found to "finish the job" (*J*, 88), despite advertisements in the national newspapers and "on the telly" until the ubiquitous Irish labourer arrives, ready and willing to complete any job once the price is right. Flanagan nails Jesus to the cross with competent ease, pockets his money and vanishes, "eschewing all displays of bravado or glamour", a professional job well done. The desacralising of Jesus' final moments purports the normality of the crucifixion at the time, inferring that its sacred status is one that has accreted over the centuries. Flanagan epitomises the concept that individuals have no control over what history will do to them and actions carried out for purely pragmatic reasons will be wholly reinterpreted by succeeding generations.

Equally, the time vortex through which the characters in the poem travel dislocates both the actuality of the historical event, inasmuch as it can have actuality, and the contemporary re-reading of that event. Flanagan's appearance as a recognisable contemporary jobber prepared to nail a man to a cross for a fee hints at contemporary moral values driven by a desire for profit at the expense of the moral outcome of that action. Time is distended in the poem, the human tragedy of Jesus' final humiliation overshadowed by a cute Irish "apparition" who elides the significance of the moment with his casual profiteering.

In his 1998 long poem *The Man Made of Rain*, Kennelly himself, rather than any voice that he chooses to operate under, is visited by "a man made of rain" (*MMR*, 15) and this gentle watery phantasm, at once liminal and utterly present, moves

freely in all dimensions, extending Judas's chronological free-
dom even further. When Lazarus emerges from his tomb, for
example, "dying for a cup of tea and a slice of Bewley's coarse-
brown" (*J*, 115), Judas takes a colour photograph of him, keep-
ing the photograph for some future posterity in a move that
satirises the furore created by the purported images of Jesus
contained in the Shroud of Turin. This contemporising of the
past by infusing it with the contemporary fetish for recording
events, serves to illustrate the divergent views aroused by the
veracity or otherwise of historical documentation.

Throughout *The Book of Judas*, Jesus' life is taped, filmed
and reported with relentless gusto by a motley crew of jour-
nalists, television crews and paparazzi and as such is subjected
to a scrutiny that should supposedly shed more light on his
personality. However, one such journalist typifies the chasing
pack, describing himself as "an opportunistic hack in a world
that's not even worth betraying" (*J*, 210) hinting at the subjec-
tive nature of much contemporary news reporting. The au-
thorial unreliability of the gospels is clearly paralleled with the
contemporary fetish for constant news updating, hinting that
the technological advances of news reporting cannot disguise
the ideologies that drive their production.

Indeed, *The Man Made of Rain* takes the chronological
freedom offered in both *Cromwell* and *The Book of Judas* to
what is in many ways its logical conclusion, despite the fact
that time itself virtually disappears as a recordable dimension
in the poem. Recovering from serious heart surgery in 1996,
Kennelly, unusually associating himself personally with the
first-person poetic voice, is visited by a figure who combines
the cool detachment, critical awareness and casual intensity
of many of Kennelly's muses. The poet's coming to terms
with the consequences of the repeated voicing of often ag-
gressive muses over the years appears to be finally telling:

I look into the eyes of the man made of rain.
I will not say I know what I see.
I will not remember, I will not forget,
I will let
Whatever happens
Happen to me,
I will let
What I know of the happy dance
Lie down with my agony.

After that, I'll see (*MMR*, 86)

Kennelly appears very much at home in the loose structure offered by the format of a themed collection of poems, exemplified in his three great epic collections, *Cromwell*, *The Book of Judas* and *Poetry My Arse*. The twelve sections of *The Book of Judas* potentially represent the twelve apostles but Kennelly is at pains in the introduction to note that the poem has only a loose claim to any kind of rigid shape, although each section has its own inherent themes and narrative drive. This flexibility is central to Kennelly's poetic composition in that his hermeneutical methodology closely reflects the ideological conclusions that can be drawn from his longer poems. If it can be said that the redeeming of the marginalised is the central theme of *The Book of Judas*, then necessarily he has to travel to these cultural, social, religious, sexual and linguistic margins in search of the energising voices that will, almost despite themselves, reveal alternative meanings to what Kennelly refers to as the "bland interchanges" (*J*, 12) that pass for everyday communication. The format's success is built on this freedom to hit and miss a constantly shifting and chimerical target, reflecting Kennelly's admission that "the flaws in my writing, which are considerable, have to do with spontaneity" (Pine, 1990: 21).

Judas does not seek to filter the voices that occupy him, often merely acknowledging their troubling presence in his dramatic existence. Because of this marginality, many of the poems in *The Book of Judas* are deeply disturbing, cascading images of brutal and casual sexuality, random and sadistic physical violence and moral turpitude. These traditionally marginalised voices play a crucial role in the process of personal signification that is undergone by Judas and their constant articulation gradually, and often dramatically, begin to paint the picture of Ireland on a much larger canvas than heretofore. This marks the crucial importance of both *Cromwell* and *The Book of Judas* in that they both seek to identify the unwieldy and complicated processes by which emergent concepts of personal and national identity emerge. In his analysis of the foundational ideologies underpinning contemporary concepts of nationhood and nation-space, Homi K. Bhabha argues convincingly that the "scraps, patches, and rags of daily life must be repeatedly turned into the signs of a national culture, while the very act of the narrative performance interpellates a growing circle of national subjects" (Bhabha, 1990: 297). This concept of a continuously shifting set of national signifiers simultaneously superseding and replacing each other in a rush away from a previously recognisable centre provides a framework within which Kennelly's long poems achieve a vital cultural significance.

Allied to his interest in a somewhat postmodern interpretation of the epic form, the signs are clearly present in his early poetry of what was to follow. Indeed, Kennelly's doctorate, awarded by Trinity College Dublin in 1966, was entitled *Modern Irish Poets and the Irish Epic* and in it he traces the development of the epic form in the work of poets such as Austin Clarke, George Russell (AE) and Yeats. *The Book of Judas*, therefore, has a long poetic genealogy and the freedom so desired by Kennelly becomes increasingly apparent as his confidence in his polyvocalism develops.

In the last poem of the collection, ironically entitled "The True Thing", Judas reflects on the inability of his language to actually express that which it purports to represent, and this is a crucial declaration that underpins many of the discussions that he engages in over the course of the book. In much the same manner as Roland Barthes described his analysis of Edgar Allen Poe's short story "Valdemar" as an "exorcism" (Lodge, 1988: 173), Kennelly's *modus operandi* in *The Book of Judas* is a minute analysis of the semiotics of communication in an attempt to expose the phantasmagorical structures at play. Barthes argues in his introduction to his piece that his fragmentation of the text will ultimately lead to a fuller understanding of the key "secondary meanings" (Lodge: 1988: 172) paralleling Kennelly's advocacy of "investigative uncertainty" (*J*, 9) in which Judas acts like a semiotic sieve, panning both the past and the present for whatever residual hermeneutical nuggets are left after the plethora of rhetorical linguistic exchanges between a wide variety of personalities, real and imagined, have been randomly dissected.

In Kennelly's text, Judas re-emerges from his biblical sojourn with a vigour and desire for articulation whetted by centuries of mute shame and his openness to debate and preparedness to encounter whatever contemporary Ireland has to throw at him supplies the collection's central dynamic. He is, however, no moral crusader, and whatever light he happens to shed on previously covered territory is often achieved with a nonchalant *sangfroid* born out of a well of distrust for the implied imperatives of human nature. Kennelly's Judas is consistent with all of Kennelly's poetic protagonists: he is a serial questioner who appears unwilling to accept anything he comes across at face value. His questions radiate like a nuclear aftershock, collapsing ideologies, opinions, beliefs, contexts and histories, and replacing them with his own "casual masterpiece":

> I am sitting here in my silence
> Listening to your silence
> Away from the streets of poison
> And the cocksure minds. (*J*, 158)

The book is dominated by recognisable themes that are recurring interests throughout Kennelly's work. The attempted voicing of the socially, historically and culturally marginalised dominates the book, from the drink-hazed Dublin outcast ozzie to a celibate James Joyce, each attempting to articulate a perspective that broadens the base upon which contemporary Irish society is to be perceived. ozzie (*sic*) dominates section two, his e.e. cummings-like non-capitalisation immediately setting both his nomenclature and his dialogues apart from the rest of the poems. His story is further complicated by the appearance of a third-party narrator, a fellow Dubliner skilled in the accurate vernacular of the inner city and his expression quickly strips away any vestige of dignity and street cred from the dismal existence of drugs, alcohol, poverty and petty crime. Echoing Leopold Bloom's discussion of national identity in Barney Kieran's pub, ozzie's take on the concept of Irish identity is somewhat more prosaic:

> ozzie herd sumwun in a pub
> sayin Ireland shud be yewnighted
> de man who did dat wud be faymuss
> ozzie was delighted. (*J*, 41)

The simplification of a complex political situation to an almost childlike desire for fame typifies ozzie's desire to exploit any opportunity for his personal economic gain. He perceives the various social, cultural and economic inequalities of contemporary Dublin as a moral *carte blanche* for what the judicial system refers to as "sundry offences" (*J*, 41) and his clearly felt sense of alienation results from a system that regards his existence as a necessary if unfortunate by-product of capitalism. ozzie, on the other hand, neither seeks nor requires the sympathy of the liberal social conscience. He is content to draw "de jesus dole in tree different playces" (*J*, 42), and apply for legal aid when his joyriding has been stopped by "de pulleece" (*J*, 42). However, as the sequence develops, it becomes clear that Kennelly's central artifice of voicing Judas through a myriad of characters is again apparent in ozzie as he questions the nature of a man whose name he expresses more often than his own:

> but everywun sez jesus dis an jesus dat
> pay de jesus rent by us a jesus pint
> till I get de jesus dole
>
> but who de jesus hell was he sez ozzie
> I dunno sez I yoor jesus iggerant sez he
> Shuv yooy iggerance up your bleedin hole. (*J*, 42)

The cover of the original 1991 Bloodaxe edition features a detail from Giotto's 1303–5 painting *The Betrayal of Christ*. The juxtaposed faces of Judas and Jesus are depicted, the former's brow fixed in a tense frown which accompanies his pursed lips while the latter's doe-like eyes gaze gently back. Jesus and Judas stare intently at each other, their eyes clearly indicating the guilt of the one and the openness of the other. It is as if they see the one in the other, both recognising that the impending kiss is a necessary element in their mutual development. The kiss physically unites them for one agonising, revelatory moment, with Jesus appearing "relieved" (*J*, 239) that Judas's actions, although ultimately signalling his eventual death, will finally set in train a series of events which will fulfil the destiny he believes is his. At the precise moment of the kiss, their eyes act as a form of Lacanian mirror, the self-image of one being reliant upon the other. Their one-dimensional gaze captures each identity in a frozen tableau of mutual recognition, the betrayer and the betrayed united in their acknowledgement of their roles and their utter interdependence.

This perspective develops Kennelly's much earlier and often explored contention that poetry operates like a "ghost compelled to return and haunt endlessly a house that symbol-

ises everything it has known and loved" (*SP* (1969), 8), indi-
cating a key ideological drive behind much of his work. The
very interdependence of Judas and Jesus indicates their unity,
as Bono notes in his essay in *This Fellow with the Fabulous Smile*
". . . if you do find Jesus, you know Judas is just around the
corner and he knows" (Persson, 1996: 13). Unfortunately for
the reader, there are few hiding places in *The Book of Judas*
and the ironic liberation offered to Judas by his kiss is that of
the accused with nothing to lose in his exposition of the du-
plicity that sought to condemn him in the first place.

The themes of mutuality can be clearly seen in *The House
That Jack Didn't Build* in which Kennelly explored the difficult
relationship between those perceived to occupy self-
proclaimed and culturally authenticated positions of authority
and those nominally and practically outside socio-cultural
spheres of influence. Kennelly's disgruntled "former occu-
pant" (*HJDB*, 14) sneers at the self-importance of Jack, a
nursery-rhyme parody character who has been evicted him
from his house. The disposed retorts:

> I am, you might say, driven,
> An impassioned simpleton
> Someone to look down on
> Someone to joke about.
> And yet
> I do not seem to fear
> Prison
> Gallows
> Rack. (*HJDB*, 15)

Here is a voice whose intensity and power is based almost
entirely upon its relationship with the evictor, strongly
suggestive of a theme in which Kennelly has long been inter-
ested. Without an evictee there can be no evictor; conse-
quently, every story of success is reliant upon a story of
failure for its very essence. Kennelly is clearly driven towards

the latter as a source of inspiration because it is largely experiences of betrayal, eviction and brutalisation that strip away the veneer of polite hermeneutics to reveal a muddied and often brutalised reality. *The Book of Judas* allows Kennelly the freedom to roam over familiar territory, rupturing the fissures in human expression and communication without the potentially stifling effect of an overt and overarching ideologically hermeneutical position. This openness to an interior questioning has always been one of Kennelly's greatest poetic strengths, but it has also been the source of some of the strongest criticism of his work.

By their nature Kennelly's epic sequences utilise a somewhat random process of selection. The events and images portrayed in many of the poems in *The Book of Judas* fall outside and between the various thematic concerns of the twelve sections but it is precisely this sense of dislocation in both the narrative structure and the process of reading that Kennelly strives for, and his stated claim in the introduction that "I have always associated unbridled, passionate muttering with freedom" (*J*, 12) permeates the collection. The book is entirely consistent with Kennelly's poetic oeuvre.

The publication of *Poetry My Arse* in 1995 marked what could be termed the final instalment of Kennelly's unofficial dialogic poetic trilogy, following on from *Cromwell* in 1983 and *The Book of Judas* in 1991. The protagonist of this collection of 546 poems, Ace de Horner, is in many ways an amalgam of the previous two historical figures, a fictional poet whose *raison d'être* appears to be to undermine and subvert the entire process that underpins the production of poetry. Of course, Kennelly had already pointed to the serious doubts he was experiencing over his personal poetic integrity in the closing stages of *The Book of Judas* when Judas, desperate to be a spokesman for something, decides that "Nothing" needs a voice. With a newfound zest, he promulgates the virtues of nothingness, but is faced by a barrage of responses from almost everyone he meets who insist they are indeed something. Judas holds his hands up in despair, declaring that "Nothing has a voice at last. Listen! Listen!" (*J*, 354). Despite this, he carries on, ignoring the clamour of a myriad of voices that insist on coming into their own through him. Their vital self-expression is, however, regarded by Judas as nothing more than an accumulation of "shite on a babbling Atlantic rock" (*J*, 355) and he describes his role in this national outpouring as nothing more than an "emetic revulsion" — a process that could equally apply to the ramblings and musings of Ace.

The diffraction of self that permeates the previous epic collections finds an almost inevitable conclusion in Ace, and a key to understanding his complex manifestations lies in the pervasive influence of Dublin, a city he describes in the introductory "Acenote" as "helplessly incestuous" (*PMA*, 13). It is a suitable acknowledgement of the importance of Dublin in the construction of Kennelly's varied poetic stages and it develops certain urban themes that played important roles in both *Cromwell* and *The Book of Judas*. Indeed, the publication of *Poetry My Arse* in 1995 was closely followed in 1996 by *Dublines*, a varied collection of Dublin-related literature, ranging from Jonathan Swift to Roddy Doyle. In this collection, co-edited with Katie Donovan, Kennelly outlines a Dublin that brims with contradictions, full of the self-righteous bravado of any capital city yet awash with self-doubt born out of a postcolonial malaise.

The voice of Judas emerges from *The Book of Judas* with an intensity, emotiveness and anger that acts like a hermeneutical Gatling-gun, spraying its emotional bullets at any target that comes into view. In the guise of a variety of hosts, from ozzie, the cider-drinking, dole-cheating Dublin petty criminal to a languid, stain-obsessed, coffee-sipping James Joyce, the narrative moves inexorably and uncomfortably over a taboo-strewn terrain, from a mother reeling over her momentary sexual desire for her twelve-year-old son (*J*, 34) to Judas's acknowledgement that his very language is the ultimate betrayer. In "Teach Me", Judas describes his language as a series of "clichés", mutterings and grunts that amount to no more than "pissing in the wind". He wonders if there is "a language on earth my use of it won't betray" and he longs for someone to "give me lessons in fidelity" although he grudgingly acknowledges that "it's hard to be true" (*J*, 357) to oneself, either emotionally or linguistically. This poem brilliantly destabilises Judas's self-reflections and adds yet another layer of ontological questioning onto the already mine-laden field of his troubled personality.

However, the poems do not shirk from voicing the socially and culturally marginalised individuals and groups who exist in the liminal spaces of Dublin society and in the course of his various dialogic exchanges Judas actively seeks out the moribund, claustrophobic and vested ideologies that drive the forces of social exclusion. Because of this, his targets are many and the voices that Judas both entertains and occupies range from a postcolonial guilt-obsessed Christopher Columbus (*J*, 317) to a skin-peeling Adolf Hitler (*J*, 231), historical figures imbued with such cultural mythology that they cease to be anything other than the reflection of the constructing culture.

However, *The Book of Judas* is a highly unstable text, constantly seeking to displace and unnerve the reader through complex and often brutal images of violence, sexual desire and linguistic dislocation. As soon as an (admittedly unsteady) pattern begins to emerge, Kennelly introduces a poem, or a series of poems, whose relation to the predominant theme appears distant and designed to upset any cosy impression that might be emerging in the reader as to the intellectual and psychological thrust of that particular section. This constant flight from order echoes Patricia Waugh's definition of postmodernism as "a pervasive crisis in the modern understanding of selfhood as founded upon a unitary coherent subjectivity" (Rice and Waugh, 1989: 346). Indeed, in the opening section entitled "Do It", the Kennelly/Judasvoice announces the maxim that will echo not only throughout the poems themselves but in the very structure that purports to hold them together: "The best way to serve the age is to betray it" (*J*, 17). Indeed, this admission that his Judas is largely incapable of expression echoes Derek Hand's analysis of John Banville's *Birchwood*:

> But a nightmarish situation still exists: writing offers a means of dealing with the past and history but it also acknowledges that all attempts at such understanding through acts of writing will necessarily fail. (Hand, 2002: 40)

In *Cromwell*, Kennelly used the variously manifested exchanges of Buffun and Oliver Cromwell as a backdrop to his social, cultural, historical and linguistic deconstruction of the origin and nature of central Irish political and cultural icons. Adopting a similar methodology in *The Book of Judas*, Kennelly liberates Judas into a form of chronological pinball in which his encounters with characters from his own life are interspersed with contemporary Irish writers and Hollywood film stars. Each stumbled-upon meeting sheds an uncertain light on the dark manifestations of self. Arguably the most energising of these encounters are the many discussions, meetings, reminiscences and bizarre dialogues that Judas has with Jesus, the one mirroring and explicating the other. Indeed, over the course of the collection, it is often difficult to identify clearly which of the two protagonists is speaking, and this dislocation works very much in Kennelly's favour as the traditional demarcation of the betrayer and the betrayed becomes blurred.

Indeed, this narrative schizophrenia neatly dovetails with the collection's advocation of the ubiquitous, non-selective and non-judgemental nature of all betrayals, the latter being a central component in any model of trust or faith, and this is a point that is well made by Anthony Roche in his excellent essay on *The Book of Judas*:

> The strength of the sequence lies in the way it builds up a circuit of betrayals in which no one case is absolute, and in which the encounter between Judas and each particular speaker is hinged around the question: "What do I care?" (Pine, 1994: 35)

This concept of a rolling betrayal encapsulates the complex relationship between Judas and Jesus that emerges from the collection. They revisit their shared historical past and both proffer explanations for their chosen behaviour, the clear emphasis being placed on the extrapolation of some kind of motives behind what appear to be increasingly unreliable and lazily interpreted models of Judas's behaviour.

Judas's monologue in the poem "Kisses" (*J*, 234), one of the most important poems in the collection, goes some way towards an exfoliation of one of the central accusations laid against Judas, namely the intimately, exquisitely gentle image of his betraying Jesus with a kiss. The image of that kiss, which adorns the cover of the collection, is one of the most important iconic religious symbols of Christianity, and Kennelly's rereading of the event from the perspective of a Judas who also exists in the contemporary world immediately redirects the focus of the kiss from its somewhat sheltered historical environs into a harsher, confused and angry contemporary realm. Indeed, the discovery of Caravaggio's missing masterpiece, *The Taking of Christ*, in the Jesuit community's Leeson Street headquarters in Dublin in 1990, added an interesting contemporary resonance to Kennelly's book and a delicious irony that one of the most celebrated images of Judas and Jesus should have been hanging in a Dublin house when it had been considered lost for over 200 years!

Judas begins his reflections by noting the lack of kissing in his life:

I have kissed but little: here and there, a mouth,
An eye, a cunt and, now and then, an arse
To ensure that I became the thing I am. (*J*, 234)

This casual, crudely sexualised contextualising of one of the most iconic moments in Christianity typifies Judas's emotional, composure, a man adroitly capable of distancing himself from any given situation thereby creating the impression that he is an almost disinterested observer of the key public events in his life. That these events have been appropriated, reinterpreted and rearticulated by a motley crew of various vested interest groups only serves to increase Judas's scepticism over the very nature of the actions that placed him in this inadvertent anti-heroic situation in the first place. His reflections on the nature of that particular kiss are compounded (a typical stylistic feature of the collection) by the appearance, in his bedsit, of one Alfonsus John O'Grady, a man who inadvertently traces the origins of his own fear of French kissing to "the first time his mother's lips kissed silk into his cheek" (*J*, 235) while Judas muses on the nature of the "spittle-orgy" that reduces the emotional suggestivity of kissing to a mere "sweaty paddling in another's flesh" (*J*, 237). Before he can settle on this reductive perspective on his actions, however, another character, a pushy novelist named Hans-Christian Wurster, leads Judas to the intriguing reflection that "One man in all this world understands that kiss", an assertion that undermines the standard biblical portrayal of that fateful moment in that Judas fails to clearly identify which of the central duo is in the dark.

Indeed, his fascinating failure to declare whether he or Jesus understood the nature of that kiss further muddies the ontological interpretation of this key event in Christian iconography. If it is indeed Jesus who understands the nature of the kiss, then Judas's role in his betrayal is exonerated as a necessary condition of the ultimate symbolism of Jesus' life, given that Judas's guilt is merely accidental in that *someone* had to betray Jesus if his messianic mission was to be realised. For Judas, it could be interpreted as merely the wrong place at the wrong time. Conversely, Kennelly's Judas is also acknowledging his confusion as to the exact role carved out for him in one of the iconic moments in the Western socioreligious paradigm. However, that status is interestingly challenged by whatever version of the gospel is consulted, given that John's gospel, for example, makes no reference to a kiss of signification, but merely recalls that Judas brought "a detachment of guards sent by the chief priests and the Pharisees" (John 18:3).

The fateful kiss, such a delicious symbol of the liminal space between love and betrayal, is therefore a far more contentious historical event than is traditionally acknowledged and Judas's calm acceptance of his complicity stems from Kennelly's portrayal of a paradoxical relationship driven more by Jesus' personal vision of his ultimate destiny than by Judas's desire to let down a man he clearly loves. If indeed we are all part of a divine plan, then Judas is aware that someone has to draw the short straw, and his subsequent historical and contemporary vilification is portrayed as clearly revelatory of the scapegoating needs of succeeding religious ideologues. Kennelly has visited this territory before and this can be clearly seen in Oliver Cromwell's description of his unwanted and unmerited role in the creation of an element of the Irish psyche that consistently seeks to blame the past for the problems of the present:

> To make me an excuse for what they
> Would fail to do, to be, being themselves". (C, 150)

In the Preface to *The Book of Judas*, Kennelly notes that he was "shocked" (J, 12) by the manifestation of the Judasvoice that questions both the veracity and integrity of the very poetry that expresses this voice. Anthony Roche notes of *The

Book of Judas that it depicts the "postmodern difficulty in distinguishing the fake from the real thing" (Pine, 1994: 109) and it is one of Kennelly's greatest strengths that it is precisely in the middle of this interpretative battlefield that he chooses to locate his work.

Conclusion

"Blitzophrenia": Brendan Kennelly's Postcolonial Vision

The poetry of Brendan Kennelly is principally characterised by various degrees and notes of resistance. From *Cast a Cold Eye* (1959) to *Martial Art* (2003), Kennelly has sought to establish a poetic independence that aggressively resists generic categorisations. At his corrosive best, Kennelly epitomises a postcolonial Irish poetics that exists on the margins, eating away at a monolithic cultural centre by consistently voicing those whose very presence begins to erode the iconographic pillars constructed to support the edifice of Irish identity. From the probings and musings of Oliver Cromwell to the carnal reflections of a bus-driving Black-and-Tan, Kennelly's poetry acts as a cultural correlative, highlighting the complex historical, social and sexual undertones that are constantly seeking an elusive expression. While Kennelly eschews overt politicisations of his work there is a discernable politico-cultural force-field within which his poetry appears to operate. Principally it involves often disturbing dialogues with a variety of both real and imagined characters who are free to explore their scapegoated roles in the fabrication of what Ernest Renan referred to as "the spiritual principle" (quoted in Bhabha, 1990: 18) of the nation. Kennelly's own description of "Blitzophrenia" (private correspondence, 1 April 1996) is the closest to a quasi-theoretical framework to which he will admit and it provides a searing and provocative lens through which an increasingly fragile and disparate contemporary Irish culture can be viewed. By this term Kennelly is referring to the multiplicity of voices struggling for expression in Buffun's psyche, rather than the traditional psychiatric condition of a dualistic schizophrenia. These voices gradually coalesce in what Kennelly refers to as the "selfswamp" (*BS*, 11) and it is precisely in the resistance to this imaginary gravitational whirlpool that Kennelly's work acquires a vital literary and cultural significance.

In the introductory essay to *Irish and Postcolonial Writing: History, Theory, Practice*, Glenn Hooper appositely notes that a good deal of contemporary Irish literature operates within "unstable and erratic boundaries" (Hooper and Graham, 2002: 12). The application of postcolonial theory to the complexities of the relationship between history and nationhood has led to the emergence of literary texts, according to Maria Tymoczko, "that question, shift, subvert and recreate cultural norms, linguistic norms and poetics" (quoted in Hooper and Graham, 2002: 182). Within these mobile parameters, Brendan Kennelly's poetry ranges over the contemporary and the historical with little concern for the temporal integrity of either, but by its very elasticity it achieves a historical insight unparalleled in contemporary Irish poetry. Given this, it is extraordinary that John Goodby, in his otherwise comprehensive book *Irish Poetry Since 1950* (2000) confines Kennelly to the briefest of occasional mentions, referring to *Cromwell* solely in an obscure aside on the contemporary use of the sonnet. This elision of the most significant contemporary poet to repeatedly deal with the complexities of Ireland's socio-cultural history is all the more inexplicable when Goodby notes that "the lack of an inclusive account of recent poetry flows from the narrowness of bilateral canonical agreements" (Goodby, 2000: 3), thereby shooting himself clearly in the canonical foot. Despite this odd critical exclusion, Kennelly's poetics clearly fulfil a crucial role in the emergence of an unstable counter-culturalism, and Terence Brown has noted the literary effects of Kennelly's chronological and temporal distension:

> An art . . . which eschews chronology is by definition a long way not only from the simple consolations and deceptions of narrative but also from any kind of stable text or unmixed mode. (Pine, 1994: 18)

It can also be argued that Kennelly's poetics, exemplified in his epic sequences, offer a far more exciting and vivid picture of the manifestations of postcolonial theory than the theory itself. While Hooper notes the importance and influence of Homi K. Bhabha's theoretical interventions and refinements of postcolonial theory in the 1990s, Kennelly was exploring precisely this territory almost a decade earlier. In his essay "DissemiNation", for example, Bhabha notes that the "political unity of the nation" is predicated upon the formation of "a signifying space that is archaic and mythical" (Bhabha, 1990: 300) whereas in the first poem of *Cromwell*, Buffun notes that his concept of national identity is built upon "a mountain of indignant legends, bizarre history, demented rumours and obscene folklore" (*C*, 15), all recognisable constituent elements of national mythologies. Kennelly's eclectic and often surreal exploration of the role of Oliver Cromwell in the formation of the Irish psyche takes him precisely to the liminal spaces Bhabha identifies as the sites of putative national signification. Indeed, in many instances in the collection, Buffun transcends both spatial and temporal boundaries in his exfoliation of self, witnessing, for example, the burning of dozens of houses by one of Cromwell soldiers, Lieutenant Girders, noting in the process "I was not born yet. But I suffer it" (*C*, 88). The freedom to roam at will through

both his personal and national histories gives Kennelly the prac-
tical opportunity to explore the contentious liminal areas of
Irish identity and to examine the originary moments of iconic
figures in the Irish consciousness. Kennelly has developed this
investigative strategy over his career, writing poems that inter-
rogate the myriad manifestations of history and language and
purport the necessity for some difficult and often disturbing
self-analysis. Judas's acknowledgement early in the collection
that "the best way to serve the age is to betray it" (_J_, 17) clearly
signals Kennelly's subversive poetic intent. Arguably, poetry
accesses these liminal areas with a clarity and freshness that
theory can only aspire to in that literary alterity provides a
narrative structure, however fractured, in which complex theo-
retical suppositions crystallise into some form of tangible ex-
perience. It would appear that postcolonial theory has been
greenhousing in Irish literature long before its much heralded
emergence in the 1980s.

The voicing of the other in Kennelly's poetry does not
elide the perception of the colonisers as greedy, violent and
arrogant oppressors but crucially it widens the aperture
through which iconographic people and events are viewed.
This widening consequently begins to erode the mythology
that inevitably attaches itself to the past, usually in the search
for an identifiable national authenticity, and it is precisely
through this methodology that Kennelly's poetry achieves its
optimum critical effectiveness.

Bibliography

Books by Brendan Kennelly

Kennelly, Brendan (1959), with Rudi Holzapfel, *Cast A Cold Eye* (Dublin: Dolmen).

Kennelly, Brendan (1961), with Rudi Holzapfel, *The Rain, The Moon* (Dublin: Dolmen).

Kennelly, Brendan (1962), with Rudi Holzapfel, *The Dark About Our Loves* (Dublin: John Augustine).

Kennelly, Brendan (1963), with Rudi Holzapfel, *Green Townlands* (Leeds: University Bibliographic Press).

Kennelly, Brendan (1963), *Let Fall No Burning Leaf* (Dublin: New Square Publications).

Kennelly, Brendan (1963), *The Crooked Cross* (Dublin: Allen Figgis).

Kennelly, Brendan (1964), *My Dark Fathers* (Dublin: New Square Publications).

Kennelly, Brendan (1965), *Up and At It* (Dublin: New Square Publications).

Kennelly, Brendan (1966), *Collection One: Getting Up Early* (Dublin: Allen Figgis).

Kennelly, Brendan (1967), *Good Souls To Survive* (Dublin: Allen Figgis).

Kennelly, Brendan (1967), *The Florentines* (Dublin: Allen Figgis).

Kennelly, Brendan (1968), *Dream of a Black Fox* (Dublin: Allen Figgis).

Kennelly, Brendan (1969), *Selected Poems* (New York: E.P. Dutton).

Kennelly, Brendan (1970), *A Drinking Cup: Poems from the Irish* (Dublin: Allen Figgis).

Kennelly, Brendan (1971), *Bread* (Dublin: Tara Telephone Publications).

Kennelly, Brendan (1971), *Selected Poems: Enlarged Edition* (New York: Dutton).

Kennelly, Brendan (ed.) (1971), *The Penguin Book of Irish Verse* (Harmondsworth: Penguin).

Kennelly, Brendan (1972), *Love Cry* (Dublin: Tara Telephone Publications).

Kennelly, Brendan (1972), *Salvation, the Stranger* (Dublin: Tara Telephone Publications).

Kennelly, Brendan (1973), *The Voices: A Sequence of Poems* (Dublin: Gallery Press).

Kennelly, Brendan (1974), *Shelley in Dublin* (Dublin: Anna Livia), reprinted in 1984 by Beaver Row Press, Dublin.

Kennelly, Brendan (1975), *A Kind of Trust* (Dublin: Gallery Press).

Kennelly, Brendan (1976), *New and Selected Poems* (Dublin: Gallery Press).

Kennelly, Brendan (1977), *Islandman: A Poem* (Dublin: Profile).

Kennelly, Brendan (1978), *A Girl: 22 Songs*, performed on RTE radio (fully published in *Breathing Spaces*, 1992).

Kennelly, Brendan (1978), *The Visitor* (Dublin: St. Bueno's).

Kennelly, Brendan (1979), *A Small Light: Ten Songs of O'Connor of Carrigafoyle* (Dublin: Gallery Press).

Kennelly, Brendan (1979), *In Spite of the Wise* (also titled *Evasions*) (Dublin: Trinity Closet Press).

Kennelly, Brendan (1980), *The Boats Are Home* (Dublin: Gallery Press).

Kennelly, Brendan (1982), *The House That Jack Didn't Build* (Dublin: Beaver Row Press).

Kennelly, Brendan (1983), *Cromwell: A Poem* (Dublin: Beaver Row Press), reprinted in 1987 by Bloodaxe Books, Newcastle-upon-Tyne.

Kennelly, Brendan (1984), *Moloney Up and At It* (Cork: Mercier).

Kennelly, Brendan (1985), *Selected Poems* (Kevin Byrne, ed.) (Dublin: Kerrymount Publications).

Kennelly, Brendan (1987), *Mary: From the Irish* (Dublin: Aisling).

Kennelly, Brendan (ed.) (1989), *Love of Ireland: Poems from the Irish* (Cork: Mercier).

Kennelly, Brendan (1990), *A Time for Voices: Selected Poems 1960–1990* (Newcastle-upon-Tyne: Bloodaxe Books).

Kennelly, Brendan (1991), *The Book of Judas* (Newcastle-upon-Tyne: Bloodaxe Books).

Kennelly, Brendan (1991), *Euripides' Medea: A New Version* (Newcastle-upon-Tyne: Bloodaxe Books).

Kennelly, Brendan (1992), *Breathing Spaces: Early Poems* (Newcastle-upon-Tyne: Bloodaxe Books).

Kennelly, Brendan (1993), *Euripides' The Trojan Women: A New Version* (Newcastle-upon-Tyne: Bloodaxe Books).

Kennelly, Brendan (ed.) (1993), *Between Innocence and Peace: Favourite Poems of Ireland* (Cork: Mercier).

Kennelly, Brendan (1994), *Journey into Joy: Selected Prose* (Åke Persson, ed.) (Newcastle-upon-Tyne: Bloodaxe Books).

Kennelly, Brendan (1995), *Poetry My Arse* (Newcastle-upon-Tyne: Bloodaxe Books).

Kennelly, Brendan (1996), *Sophocles' Antigone: A New Version* (Newcastle-upon-Tyne: Bloodaxe Books).

Kennelly, Brendan (1996), *Lorca's Blood Wedding: A New Version* (Newcastle-upon-Tyne: Bloodaxe Books).

Kennelly, Brendan (ed. with Katie Donovan) (1996), *Dublines* (Newcastle-upon-Tyne: Bloodaxe Books).

Kennelly, Brendan (1998), *The Man Made of Rain* (Newcastle-upon-Tyne: Bloodaxe Books).

Kennelly, Brendan (1998), *The Singing Tree* (Newcastle-upon-Tyne: Bloodaxe Books).

Kennelly, Brendan (1999), *Begin* (Newcastle-upon-Tyne: Bloodaxe Books).

Kennelly, Brendan (2001), *Glimpses* (Newcastle-upon-Tyne: Bloodaxe Books).

Kennelly, Brendan (2002), *The Little Book of Judas* (Newcastle-upon-Tyne: Bloodaxe Books).

Kennelly, Brendan (2003), *Martial Art* (Newcastle-upon-Tyne: Bloodaxe Books).

Books, Theses and Articles about Brendan Kennelly

Hederman, Mark Patrick (1984), "The Monster in the Irish Psyche" (*Irish Literary Supplement*, Autumn).

Longley, Edna (1984), "Beyond the Incestuous Irish Anger" (*Fortnight*, May).

Otto, Erwin (1976), *Das Lyrische Werk Brendan Kennelly* (Frankfurt am Main: Peter Lang).

Persson, Åke (ed.) (1996), *This Fellow with the Fabulous Smile: A Tribute to Brendan Kennelly* (Newcastle-upon-Tyne: Bloodaxe Books).

Persson, Åke (2000), *Betraying the Age: Social and Artistic Protest in Brendan Kennelly's Work* (Gothenburg: University of Gothenburg Press).

Pine, Richard (1994), *Dark Fathers into Light: Brendan Kennelly, Bloodaxe Critical Anthologies: 2* (Newcastle-upon-Tyne: Bloodaxe Books)

Sedlmayr, Gerold (2003), "'Drawing Breath Somewhere between Stars and Skeletons': Brendan Kennelly's Literary Works" (Unpublished PhD thesis, University of Passau, Germany).

Interviews and Correspondence

Carty, Ciaran (1981), interview with Brendan Kennelly, 8 February, *Sunday Independent.*

Holzapfel, Rudi (1990), interview with John McDonagh.

Murphy, Daniel (1987), interview with Brendan Kennelly (entitled *Education and the Arts: A Research Report*) published by the School of Education of Trinity College, Dublin.

Pine, Richard (1990), "Q&A. with Brendan Kennelly" in *The Irish Literary Supplement*, Spring, pps. 21–23.

Private unpublished correspondence, 1 April 1996; letter in possession of current author.

Kennelly, Brendan (1989), interview with magazine *Alpha*, 28 September.

Other Works Cited

Abbott, Wilber (1939), *The Writings and Speeches of Oliver Cromwell, Volume 2: 1649–1653* (Cambridge, MA: Harvard University Press).

Abercrombie, Lascalles (1922), *The Epic: An Essay* (London: Martin Secker).

Anderson, Benedict (1983), *Imagined Communities* (London: Verso).

Barthes, Roland (1997), *Mythologies* (London: Vintage).

Beckett, J.C. (1966), *The Making of Modern Ireland, 1603–1923* (London: Faber and Faber).

Bhabha, Homi K. (1990), *Nation and Narration* (London: Routledge).

Bhabha, Homi K. (1994), *The Location of Culture* (London: Routledge).

Bourke, Angela (1999), *The Burning of Brigid Cleary* (London: Pimlico).

Bradshaw, Brendan (1994), "Nationalism and Historical Scholarship" in Ciaran Brady (ed.), *Interpreting Irish History* (Dublin: Irish Academic Press).

Brown, Terence (1991), "British Ireland", in Edna Longley (ed.), *Culture in Ireland: Division or Diversity?* (Belfast: Institute of Irish Studies, Queen's University).

Cairns, David and Shaun Richards (1988), *Writing Ireland: Colonialism, Nationalism and Culture* (Manchester: Manchester University Press).

de Paor, Liam (1986), *The Peoples of Ireland* (London: Hutchinson and Co.).

Dickens, Charles (1977), *Hard Times* (St. Albans: Panther Books).

Eagleton, Terry (1983), *Literary Theory: An Introduction* (Oxford: Basil Blackwell).

Farrell, Brian (ed.) (1973), *The Irish Parliamentary Tradition*, Dublin: Gill and Macmillan.

Ferguson, John (1972), *A Companion to Greek Tragedy* (Austin: University of Texas Press).

Foster, R.F. (1988), *Modern Ireland, 1600–1972* (London: Penguin).

Foster, R.F. (1993), *Paddy and Mr Punch* (London: Penguin).

Fraser, Antonia (1973), *Cromwell: Our Chief of Men* (London: Weidenfeld and Nicholson).

Freud, Sigmund (1954), *The Interpretation of Dreams* (London: George Allen and Unwin).

Garvin, Tom (1987), *Nationalist Revolutionaries in Ireland: 1858–1928* (Oxford: Clarendon Press).

Goodby, John (2000), *Irish Poetry Since 1950: From Stillness into History* (Manchester: Manchester University Press).

Graham, Colin (1994), in *The Irish Review*, No. 16.

Hand, Derek (2002), *John Banville: Exploring Fictions* (Dublin: The Liffey Press).

Heaney, Seamus (1966), *Death of a Naturalist* (London: Faber).

Heaney, Seamus (1969), *Door Into the Dark* (London, Faber).

Heaney, Seamus (1980), *Preoccupations: Selected Prose, 1968–1978* (London: Faber and Faber).

Hollander, John and Frank Kermode (eds.) (1973), *The Oxford Anthology of English Literature: The Literature of Renaissance England* (Oxford: Oxford University Press).

Hooper, Glenn and Colin Graham (eds.) (2002), *Irish and Postcolonial Writing: History, Theory, Practice* (Basingstoke: Palgrave Macmillan).

Hyde, Douglas (1899), *A Literary History of Ireland* (London: T. Fisher Unwin).

Jones, Alexander (ed.) (1968), *The Jerusalem Bible* (London: Darton, Longman and Todd).

Kavanagh, Patrick (1984), *Patrick Kavanagh: The Complete Poems* (ed. Peter Kavanagh) (Newbridge: The Goldsmith Press).

Keane, John B. (1990), *Three Plays* (Cork: The Mercier Press).

Keegan, Paul (ed.) (2000), *The New Penguin Book of English Verse* (London: Penguin).

Kiberd, Declan (1995), *Inventing Ireland: The Literature of the Modern Nation* (London: Jonathan Cape).

Lefevre, Andre (1992), *Translation/History/Culture: A Sourcebook* (London: Routledge).

Lloyd, David (1993), *Anomalous States* (Dublin: Lilliput Press).

Lodge, David (ed.) (1988), *Modern Criticism and Theory: A Reader* (Harlow: Longman).

Longley, Edna (1991), *Culture in Ireland: Division or Diversity?* (Belfast: Institute of Irish Studies, Queen's University).

Martin, Augustine (ed.) (1987), *An Anthology of Short Stories* (Dublin: Gill and Macmillan).

Mishra, Vijay and Bob Hodge (1993), "What is Postcolonialism?" in Patrick Williams and Laura Chrisman (eds.), *Colonial Discourse and Post-Colonial Theory*, Hemel Hempstead: Harvester Wheatsheaf, pp. 276–91.

Morrill, John (1993), *The Nature of the English Revolution* (London: Longman).

Moynihan, Maurice (ed.) (1980), *Speeches and Statements by Eamon de Valera 1917–1973* (Dublin: Gill and Macmillan).

Ngugi, Wa Thiong'o (1986), *Decolonising the Mind: The Politics of Language in African Literature* (London: James Curry).

O'Toole, Fintan (1994), *Black Hole, Green Card* (Dublin: New Island Books).

Quinn, Antoinette (1991), *Patrick Kavanagh: Born-Again Romantic* (Dublin: Gill and Macmillan).

Rice, Philip and Patricia Waugh (1989), *Modern Literary Theory* (London: Arnold).

Said, Edward (1991), *Orientalism* (London: Penguin).

Said, Edward (1993), *Culture and Imperialism* (London: Chatto and Windus).

Vellacott, Ian (trans. and ed.) (1963), *Euripides: Medea/Hecabe/Electra/Heracles* (Harmondsworth: Penguin, 1963).

Woolrych, Austin (1970), "Oliver Cromwell and the Rule of the Saints" in R.H. Parry (ed.), *The English Civil War and After* (London: Macmillan).

Index